Possibility
Mind
Shift

The Practice of Living in Possibility!

Anita Bakker and Hilary Drummond

Balboa Press books may be ordered through booksellers or by contacting:

Balboa Press
A Division of Hay House
1663 Liberty Drive
Bloomington, IN 47403
www.balboapress.com
844-682-1282

Cover art was designed by Joanna Grant. @JoannaGrantArt   www.joannagrant.com

Interior Image Credit: Hilary Drummond, Anita Bakker, Leza MacDonald

ISBN: 978-1-9822-5898-6 (sc)
ISBN: 978-1-9822-5899-3 (e)

Library of Congress Control Number: 2020922823

Print information available on the last page.

Balboa Press rev. date: 12/17/2020

BALBOA.PRESS
A DIVISION OF HAY HOUSE

Possibility Mind Shift

The Practice of Living in Possibility!

Forward

Imagine living a life just a little bit better than it is now, and then a little better, and even better than you thought! Go on, visualize it in your head. Your home is just a bit more comfy, happy and really "yours" whether it's a cabin in the woods or a condo in a high-rise. You do work that you find more fulfilling and interesting and have a circle of friends who stimulate you and hold you close. All of it is satisfying, comfortable and FUN! Okay maybe not everything, but certainly the larger portion of it. Imagine all the different components of that life coming together into a whole, allowing you to really live into your own dream. Sound impossible? *We don't think so!*

For years we've worked with clients helping them get closer to the life that seems so hard to reach. We've seen clients courageously reach out for the imaginary trapeze, grab the bar, and take the steps that will bring them closer each day to what they really long for in their lives. **Possibility Mind Shift or PMS** is a tool to help you get there in an interesting, fun, and systematic manner. **PMS** has grown into the book you hold in your hand. Real stories, years of research, working with clients and learning in our own lives has helped us to prepare this living document. You can do it once, or many times learning more each time you review it. We hope you learn, stretch and have fun.

Go ahead.

You know you want to. Come with us and....

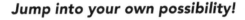

Jump into your own possibility!

Acknowledgements

So many people have been involved in making this book a reality. We'd like to thank all those who participated in our workshops and used **PMS** in the different formats we have developed over the years. Many have given feedback and shared their ideas on how to make it richer and more user friendly. Of special note is Phyllis Nieman who proofed and edited the last two versions making our writing better and helping us clarify what we really wanted to say…*in our own way*. There were many others who contributed including: Lindsay Allan, Marion Boyd, Joanna Grant, Lisa Lauze, Misha Marechal, Laura Messenger, and Wendi Wright, who read all the modules and gave us valuable suggestions. We, however, take full responsibility for any errors not found and corrected!

A- Anita

It is with profound gratitude that I thank my late parents, Peter and Olivia Keryluke who were ahead of their time, modelling a coach approach to develop our critical thinking skills. They effectively used every experience as a learning moment to question, challenge, learn and enjoy. I have deep appreciation and thanks for my sister Tanya Swaren who, in addition to being my life long best friend, altered the course of my career when she developed a program called Survival Skills for the 21st Century that I feel privileged to have facilitated and which helped lay the groundwork for me to pursue Coaching as a profession. I'm so grateful for my children, Cam, Janelle and Curtis who taught me more than they could imagine and who have become wonderful parents to my six beautiful grandchildren who also now continue to teach me how to navigate in this changing world. I am also full of gratitude to my long-time dear friend and golf/travel buddy, MJ Charman who kept me sane through tough times, helped me learn to call a spade a spade and keeps me laughing a lot! I am thankful and have a deep appreciation for Steve Lewis, the man in my life who is so wise, funny, loving and kind, and who supports me in all my projects and hobbies. There are many more people who I could fill multiple pages with…thank you to my BAGS Sisters, the Summerland Seven and my brother Ben Keryluke (that 100% hellion I refer to in this book turns out to be quite the opposite now…pretty sure there's some "angel" in him!) who has been my learning buddy since we were adventurous young kids and continues to be now as he, along with his wife Marilyn, parents their two beautiful young grandchildren. You are an inspiration!

H- Hilary

I would like to acknowledge the support from my late parents, Jim and Lillian Drummond, for providing me with the foundation on which to grow and challenge the world. They provided ongoing support and modelled how important books and life long learning are; a value I continue to embrace. I am pleased to add to the family library of authors. Tom Walsh, my husband of over 35 years, has supported me in my quest as an entrepreneur, something I would never have considered if he hadn't modelled that in his own life. He has held the fort at home for years as I went off to courses and retreats, laughingly calling me "Runaround Suzie". Our marriage has never been boring and I have felt supported and challenged over the years. I would like to thank my sons, Ian, Dean and Isaac who continue to provide me with new ways to look at the world. I have grown more as a person because I am their mother. I owe much to my dear friends who have been there for me over the years in a variety of roles; listening, talking, being and doing. Each of you has added something to my life and learning. I am grateful for my musical buddies who support me in my musical endeavors and add more levity, passion and joy to my life. And I am grateful for all I have learned from the many clients and patients I have worked with over the past 43 years, often at great times of trial in their lives. They opened their homes and often their hearts to me allowing me to help them get closer to the lives they wanted.

Together, we'd like to thank all our family members and friends who have been involved in our growth and journeys over the years (which, we're pretty sure must have been frustrating at times!). They are featured in many of the true stories in this book...along with the personal photos we've shared with you! We are fortunate to have found each other; having fun while working together has been such an amazing experience, reinforced every time we looked at something the same way, said the same thing at the same time or laughed at our own foolishness. Our friendship has grown as we clarified our meanings, had the tough conversations and drilled down to make this product as rich as it could possibly be.

Finally, we want to thank every woman who has ever taken a step to make her own life richer and better. Each journey begins with a single step, no matter how small, and the courage of every one of you keeps us in awe.

Table of Contents

Welcome to
Possibility
Mind Shift

We're in this together! Meet your learning partners, Anita and Hilary…they both highly value (in this order!) fun, learning, thinking and growing. They invite you to come on this **PMS** journey to enrich the lives you are living. It's all about the voyage and it's all about you, so be ready to work with us to coauthor this as your own book. Where did this start? Well, here's an overview…

Anita chose marriage and children early in her life and through a temporary job with the Alberta Government stumbled into becoming an adult educator. That journey lead to a long and successful career as a self-employed consultant, career facilitator and executive coach. She lived her life in happenstance, finding work she loved by chance, then going to College and University to gain knowledge and credibility. Anita's background is rounded out with an Erma Bombeck style "Doctorate in Life", earned through a long-term marriage, three wonderfully patient and forgiving adult children and six beautiful grandchildren! This includes specialization in laughter, sorrow, love and continuous deep reflective learning. She grew up in Edmonton, Alberta and moved to the beautiful Okanagan Valley in B.C. in 1992.

Hilary has had a long career as an occupational therapist. She worked in a variety of settings and in 1986 started one of the longest standing occupational therapy private practices in British Columbia. Throughout the years she has pursued personal growth and professional education; both areas are core values to her and often overlap. Over the years Hilary realized that every little step she took to increase her self-understanding helped in every area of her life. Each step lead to another and the change was gradual but profound. Then she discovered coaching and was exposed to a language and a process that fit into her values and beliefs like the perfect puzzle piece. Hilary also lives in the Okanagan valley in southern British Columbia, Canada. She has lived a life that includes a long marriage, raising three sons to become wonderful young men, learning how to play as well as work, and always making fun a priority.

When Anita and Hilary connected in the early 2000's it felt like a long friendship rediscovered. As they started working together, they realized how similar their values were. They both loved learning and helping others learn…and it had to include laughing, music and having fun! They both were passionate about the possibility of helping other women have richer and more satisfying lives. Over time and the development of a variety of workshops and projects the first edition of **Possibility Mind Shift** or "**PMS**" was born.

For most, we recognize that the acronym **PMS** represents something that can have a negative connotation as hormone changes can alter who we are and how we interact in the world. We also recognize that continuous learning and growing takes place not just in good times, but more often when we are challenged and struggle. In fact, as we looked back on our lives to find the stories with the biggest impact, we discovered our best learning occurred while in a lowered threshold for managing our emotions; and isn't that what happens when experiencing physiological pms symptoms?

The selection of this acronym is in keeping with our desire to have fun and laugh at ourselves and circumstances. The choice of "pms", something often fraught with negative emotion, helps us maintain our sense of humour and view "tough times" through the lens of self-awareness and growth.

Growth usually happens in an uncomfortable way and pms is no exception to that rule. So, it is with no disrespect that we use this acronym, our intention is to reinforce that learning can be uncomfortable…but oh so much sweeter when we can get through it, past it and grow stronger because of it.

So even if the idea of "that" pms is unpleasant to you, consider taking this first step into a new way of looking at it and at your life, and challenge yourself to laugh at both yourself and the circumstances while you grow more beautiful, more human and more able to develop into whatever challenges come your way.

The purpose of this **PMS** process is to create a manageable system that helps you hold yourself accountable in small bites while using your life and your environment for real-time learning. That's SMALL bites in **big** capital letters! That means, take your time and don't just read, but DO! Do self-assess, do dig deeper, do watch how you are being, what you are doing and how others are reacting to you and interacting with you. In fact, do get someone close to you (that you trust and respect) to give you feedback…and don't get mad at them if it's feedback you don't particularly like!

We often say people are fascinating. Well, our reactions to others are equally fascinating, so pay attention to yourself; your own process, reactions, and observations to get the most out of this.

PMS is a process that can be applied to any situation in life. We have experienced many different phases of life and will tell stories about them and how they helped us grow; sometimes not in a very pleasant or easy manner. Whether you are a new mom, in the middle of your busy career and life, or considering retirement there will be something here for you! Identify the kernels of truth that speak to you and apply them to your current situation.

> *"The future comes one day at a time."*
> *Dean Acheson*

It's time to focus on what you CAN DO, what you CAN MANAGE, what you CAN CHANGE and how you CAN GROW into the possibility you believe in, in your work and in your life.

This program is designed to guide you through your own self-discovery process. There will be stories, questions (tough ones sometimes) and "treasure hunts" or field studies (these simply mean looking, seeking, questioning, reflecting, journaling and learning). You will be challenged to see yourself in action and interaction. Notice what you notice (with no judgment); identify gifts, talents and challenges; and create the vision of the possibility you would like to grow into.

Each week builds on the next and provides a firm foundation to integrate with the next topic.

Every one of us can live a better life, but to do that we need to step out of our unconscious habits and conditioning, pay attention to values and satisfiers and move intentionally into a more rewarding possibility that we each design for ourselves. **So, get ready, get set…. GROW!!!**

POSSIBILITY MIND SHIFT PROCESS CHECKLIST
This is **your** process…the more you put into it the more you'll get out of it!
Here's how to get started…

❑ Remember this is a **process** that takes time…slowly progress through the modules, (completing… no, **savouring** no more than one module a week), allocate the time to carefully consider and ponder the ideas and stories in these pages. How do they apply to your life? Remember to stop at the end of each module. If you feel compelled to do more, just dig deeper into the subject in that segment. You might ask yourself a number of questions to ensure you obtain the maximum benefit of that module. Some of those questions may be:

   o Why did I answer that way?
   o What is meaningful about that?
   o Why is that important to me? *Or…why isn't that important to me?!!!*
   o What did I not consider or what might I have missed?
   o What would someone I really admire and respect think about this?
   o Is what I am thinking true? Is it a fact or a perception?

❑ Use the pages in this book to **journal** your thoughts, ponder the questions or just reflect on your process. (*Even if you don't write a lot, jot down some key words or for the more creative and visual, you might draw pictures, glue pictures from magazines, or make note of a song that represents your thoughts and feelings!*). **Co-author this book**…make it your own. We have given you some questions in the journal pages but don't limit yourself to just those. Ask your own questions as you work your way through what really matters to you.

❑ When you encounter new information, carefully consider and perhaps re-read it for reflection and a deeper understanding. When the questions are asked, **don't stop** with your **first** answer or response – did we already say this? Well we're saying it again because it's really important. Ask yourself:

   o *Why you chose that response?*
   o *What is beneath that answer?*
   o *Why do you think that? Is that the truth?*

Dig deeper…learn more. Your real learning is just a layer or two below your first response or where you are right now!

❑ **Notice** when you are inspired and interested in a topic and notice when your interest wanes. *What does that mean to you?* **Paying attention** to how you respond can combine your emotion and motivation and be an indicator of what you have learned.

❑ An additional module at the end of the book provides you with more field studies or treasure hunts to consider. If you really want to dive deeper into your learning, don't move forward into the next module. Choose an exercise, idea or research project from our last module and look at it from the perspective of where you are right now.

MAKE IT EVEN BETTER...Invite a friend (or your Coach) to take this learning journey with you and enjoy the benefits of a shared experience. Then **make a promise** to your learning partner to commit to each other and yourself. Share your own stories and perspectives, ask each other questions and celebrate when you have a breakthrough moment.

Most of all, have fun!
Enjoy this process and change your life one week at a time!

Week 1
Checking Your Temperature

We can all learn from anything, from anyone, anywhere, anytime...**if** there's a level of awareness and openness. It has been said that a fish doesn't see its own water just like we don't see our own circumstances. Often, we're so absorbed in our daily lives that we miss important signs of what is really happening in our lives. Our eyes only see outward, so of course it's easy for us to see the behaviour of others and "know" what they should do. Yet the most important person for us to observe is our self to live the fullest life possible – after all, *we can't change anyone else, we can only change ourselves.*

So, get ready to learn from fish and frogs, people and things, and most of all yourself. Think about this parable, because frogs can teach us great life enhancing lessons!

Imagine a frog jumping into boiling water...it will leap straight out to save its life. But imagine a frog springs into a pot of cool water on a heat source and the temperature of that water is being gradually increased. That frog will slow with fatigue as the temperature rises, continuing to paddle with diminishing energy until it succumbs to that increased heat and total exhaustion.

This parable reminds us that we are hard-wired to respond to immediate threats to our survival but a gradual change can be just as insidious and dangerous. It will slowly, over time and circumstances, sap our energy and drain our reserves.

We need to *NOTICE* our discomfort rather than avoid it.

The cost of avoiding gradual discomfort can lead to unhealthy choices and addictions that include alcohol, drugs, overwork and stress. The "superhero" drive to do everything and to do it best continues to thrive. The hero status feeds stress as the dependence grows into a pattern of negative behaviour.

"Heroes" become preoccupied with crisis, providing a convenient excuse for limiting behaviours that includes less time and attention for family, friends, fun and self. This behaviour is an example of the "boiled frog" syndrome where we forget what it feels like to be happy and fulfilled. It's nearly impossible to break these habits unless we intentionally pull out of the water we are swimming in, assess the temperature, and examine the heat sources. Only then are we able to make the appropriate adjustments.

We spend a lot of energy meeting our challenges and being concerned about politics, other people and what others think about us. If we put that energy to better use, it may be a start to lowering the heat in our lives. Our external environment and our worries sometimes seem to be eating us up. If we change some of our behaviours, attitudes, self-talk and actions we will cause a shift that takes a good chomp out of our worries!

What might you do to positively influence your life through a shift to courage, positive self-talk, action and changed behaviours?

 Over many years, my husband was extremely ill with diabetes, heart and kidney disease. I was primarily a caregiver during that time. As much as I needed to be there for him, I found that I was losing myself in that role. I realized that I needed to take care of myself but didn't know how. I didn't even know what I liked for myself anymore…I had forgotten who I was.

Through a coaching process, the question was asked of me "what did you love to do when you were a kid?" I remembered that I loved singing, music, dancing and sports. I had been playing my guitar at home alone all along, but this realization highlighted my need for socialization.

I reached deep into my courage and stepped through my fear to audition for a singing group and booked a golf lesson (both things I wasn't all that good at!)…and those two things have been feeding my soul through the last years of my husband's illness, his death and the regrowth into my new life.

We can use lots of excuses that form barriers and create the "safety of becoming a victim" of our circumstances. Or we can choose to break through those barriers to something better, even within the limitations of those conditions. Find and use your strength and successes. An example of this positive shift is the true story of an 80-year-old woman who had to move from her home but could only afford rent of under $1,000 per month. There was nothing available at that price but rather than become a victim of her circumstances, and after many attempts to find what she needed, she made an appointment to talk to the mayor of her city. Through that gutsy move she found exactly what she needed with a year lease in a local motel for $750 per month. Many would have become a victim of those circumstances, but she courageously took control. If she had just complained, circumstances would have left her homeless.

 At a meeting set up for a group of people planning an excursion together, I found myself reacting in an angry manner to a man who had taken over the planning meeting. His wife had done most of the work to date and it felt like he was pushing her out of the way and not letting her talk. I got a little snarky with him and then recalled many occasions in my young adulthood where I had felt men either disregarded or belittled me because I was a woman.

I was puzzled by my reaction. I couldn't really think of a reason why I would respond in that manner. It was easier to think the guy was a jerk! A few days later it hit me that in my family of origin, the boys were much more highly valued than the girls. I had grown up knowing that my brother, just because he was a boy, had more value to my parents. No wonder I reacted the way I did. Understanding this has taken some of the angst out of dealing with more aggressive men. It had limited my success in situations where I didn't recognize what was happening, allowing my emotion to inappropriately influence my actions. I now recognize my own self-worth without the need to feel protective when challenged by men. I can address the issue at hand without the emotional charge. However, I had

to stop and carefully consider how to react. Had I not learned that lesson I would have continued to simply respond to the man's behaviour rather than taking responsibility for my emotional response. Another great lesson learned and an awakening!

In his book "*Simplicity and Success*", Bruce Elkin uses the analogy of living our lives as if we were a train; moving straight ahead, pushing through with no ability to change direction or make a turn. On a train trip you know exactly where your starting and finishing points are, what area you will travel through, how long it will take and all the stops in between. It is predictable and fixed.

Consider what the differences would be if you lived your life as if you were on a sailboat. You know where you are starting and where you want to end up, but your route will vary depending on the tides and the weather. You may encounter storms, mechanical difficulties, other boats or a variety of other factors that will determine your destiny. Instead of following a fixed and detailed plan the individual has to be flexible, dealing with change and circumstances as they occur. If blown off course, you can use tools to determine your current position and make the necessary corrections to end up where you want to be. Compare this to what happens when a train goes off the track!! Is your life more like a train on tracks (or off the tracks?!) or a sailboat on the ocean?

Perhaps this analogy can be applied to life. Like a sailor, have clear objectives (your destination) in mind and check regularly to ensure you are remaining on course. Remain focused on your goal and have the flexibility to make the necessary changes as dictated by circumstance. Similar to a sailor, do what you need to do in order to get to your destination. How do you live your life every day? As a sailor or a railroad engineer?

History has been captured by writers who happened upon others busy living their lives. Lives that made good stories in the journey of humankind. They were people just like you and me who shared experiences that others found interesting or important.

When I went back to University after two decades away from school, I was scared and intimidated. I didn't feel like I belonged as I had little to offer. A friend and colleague changed my perspective dramatically. She suggested that all the students in that postgraduate program were simply people engaged in a learning process with others who had previous experience with the subject. Those who had written books, created theories and engaged in spirited debates have become the classmates of the current students regardless of when they took part in this learning journey and what their position was.

Each person was contributing their own perspectives and experience to a respectful discussion of the various ideas brought forward over time and distance. I could question, contribute and advance my personal opinion unencumbered by my feelings of inadequacy. And it isn't done yet. This whole process will continue with the addition of succeeding generations of learners and contributors.

You are a part of the history of people, indeed of the world and the universe! If each of us thought about the importance of our role in history, we might live our lives in a manner that created a more meaningful and positive contribution to the story.

Reflections and Guiding Questions...

So, let's examine your water......

In the box on the right using a scale of 1 – 10 (10 being AWESOME!!) enter the number that ☐ you think best represents your level of life satisfaction right now........................

Think hard this week as you move through each day. What do you notice about your life, your relationships, and your feelings? Reflect on the questions on the following journal pages to create an enhanced awareness of yourself and the "water you are swimming in"!

Keep in mind that it's much easier to blame our emotions, circumstances or other people for the temperature of our water. Considering we have minimal control over the actions of others, we might as well have a look at ourselves and see what changes we can make to our own behaviour.

Let's stop kissing frogs in the search for Prince Charming and take stock of our own life! The only person we really have any control over is our self!

What would your life look like at the ideal temperature?

....

....

....

....

....

....

....

....

....

....

....

....

....

....

....

....

....

....

....

....

....

....

....

What are some habits or behaviours that might be contributing to uncomfortable temperatures?

....

....

....

....

....

....

....

....

....

....

....

....

....

....

....

....

....

....

....

....

....

....

....

....

What are the heat sources you really need to deal with?

....

....

....

....

....

....

....

....

....

*It may be hard, but please **STOP** right here, right now!*

*This isn't a novel…it's your life! To get the most from this process, stop here for a week. If you still want to read, check out **Module 21** for questions and activities to deepen your experience! Most importantly, pause, think, question, ponder and gather new perspectives on yourself and your life. You might want to recall and write your own stories that support or challenge the concepts in this module. Or call that friend or Coach you're working with to talk this through… it's surprising what speaking your own words out loud will do for your ability to hear yourself!*

*After all, that's where **PMS** came from…our own experiences, awareness and discussions.*

Hmmmmm…Could moving too fast be one of the habits

that turns the temperature up on your water?

They say... *"Put your money where your mouth is."*
We say... *"Put your time and energy where your values are."*

Values are at the core of every decision we make, the jobs we prefer, the geographic areas we live in, the partners we choose and ultimately the status of our health. When we experience conflict in our values the symptoms can be surprising and disturbing, from low energy and edginess to serious medical problems.

According to Webster's New World Dictionary...values are defined as *"a thing or quality having intrinsic worth"*, or as a *"set of beliefs or standards"*. Values have a huge impact on our lives, whether we are aware of it or not.

Think of a specific incident when you felt most valued, perhaps a day at work, at home, or volunteering. It was likely a time when you were fully engaged in an activity, and time passed so quickly you may have even missed a meal or a break! As you recall details of the occasion consider what you believe were some core values key to that event. Conversely, you may remember a particular instance when you were frustrated, agitated or angry and upset with yourself or others. Likely you had a values conflict. If you carefully consider the incident you might identify some values that were being violated.

I had a values conflict. I was a health professional who had been taught that I had to "help" the people I worked with. When I moved into private practice, I knew the people who were paying me to work with the injured clients I was seeing also wanted to see results such as helping people get back to work. I knew if I didn't perform well and make a difference in how long people were off work, or how much paid support service they got for a long period of time, I was unlikely to keep getting referrals. I thought hard about how I could work within my own personal values, continue to get referrals and make a difference to the folks I was seeing every day.

*I loved being an occupational therapist and valued building relationships with the people that I worked with and yet it seemed if I didn't focus on the monetary values of the insurance companies I would not be in business for long. I wrote a list of the values that were the most important to me in life and in work (they tend to be the same)! I then made myself a small book with a core value on each page and a description of how I would "**Live**" that value. Then, throughout the work day I made a note when something happened to me that demonstrated that value. I wrote down even the simplest thing that helped me identify when I was living the values I cherished. Eventually it wasn't necessary to record the actions as I became more aware of opportunities to "walk my talk". This helped me measure my progress in maintaining consistency between my values and the expectations of the insurance companies.*

What are the values you cherish and want to bring into your work?

 When I was a young mom, I took a part time job as a receptionist for a local doctor. I loved my work, greeting patients and making them feel comfortable. The doctor I worked with gradually increased my responsibilities. I embraced these opportunities to learn and become a more integral part of his team. I felt valued and trusted as he began to rely on me for more procedures.

This progressed to me assisting with small medical procedures. Soon he had me gowned and assisting with vasectomies!!! When I told my friends what I was doing at work, they found it hysterically funny. However, the more I talked (and joked) about it, the more uncomfortable I felt about the situation. There was no doubt that some of my values were being realized in spades; I was learning and helping others while gaining the confidence of the doctor in a work environment I enjoyed. But it wasn't long before I found myself worrying and losing sleep over the situation. Something was wrong. I was clearly living in a values conflict. I did not have the medical training for this work. This was unethical and a serious violation of health care standards and my integrity. Strangely, the humour in telling this story nurtured one of my primary values of "fun", yet as I retold the story, I became aware of a contradiction between the two values of "fun" and "respect". This situation clearly wasn't respectful of either the patients or the nurses who should have been fulfilling this role.

Values Clarification

From the following list, choose the words that best describe your top 8 values.
Feel free to add any others that aren't on this list.

	Creativity		Freedom		Leadership
	Security		Personal growth		Learning
	Education		Love		Independence
	Challenge		Empowerment		Passion
	Spirituality		Inner harmony		Adventure
	Comfort		Honesty		Intelligence
	Integrity		Family		Aesthetics
	Respect		Productivity		Societal contribution
	Achievement		Health		Joy
	Courage		Intimacy		Environment
	Friendship		Fitness		Play
	Arts		Autonomy		Competition
	Belonging		Culture		Excitement
	Hard work		Inclusion		Harmony
	Reputation		Innovation		Personal Mastery
	Quality		Recognition		Self-respect
	Wealth		Growth		Wisdom
	Conservation		Responsibility		Loyalty
	Power		Fame		Purity
	Competence		Cooperation		Peace
	Change		Community		Serenity
	Status		Order		

As you consider the values that you have identified which four are the most important to you, in order of preference.

1._____

2._____

3._____

4._____

> *"Happiness is a state of consciousness,*
> *which proceeds from the achievement of one's values."*
> ~Ayn Rand~

Some people become overwhelmed when trying to decide the three or four values that are most important to them. Others find this process relatively easy.

Those exposed to different experiences and backgrounds who have had their values tested throughout their lifetime will naturally find it easier to identify and articulate them. Others may find it more challenging. However difficult it is, don't give up; the rewards are worth the effort. Decisions and choices will become clearer and overall life satisfaction greater once you clearly define and articulate your values. It's a strong step towards a purposeful life.

As you take more time this week examining your values, consider the definitions of the words you are choosing to represent them. Definitions are **very** important to consider as you move through this exercise. You don't need a dictionary for this, just trust your own understanding. For example, one participant stated that she could not have inner harmony without integrity, respect, and authenticity. Harmony was her most important value but it could not exist for her without the other three. Knowing this makes it easier to understand how we make decisions and how our value system affects us in our daily life.

When you consider your values, also think about what is holding you back from living them. Many of us are limited by the way we think. In his leadership book, the *"Art of Possibility"*, Ben Zander presents some simple concepts that if applied to our lives can drastically change how we look at things and ultimately affect the outcomes. One of the concepts Zander presents is how we grade ourselves and others, inadvertently limiting the possibility of what we can achieve. How many times have you thought that you are not good enough for the job you really want, or not talented enough to get that plum assignment? If we give ourselves that message, it will become our reality.

Mr. Zander told all his university music students at the beginning of the school year that they could all achieve an A in his class. He asked each one to write a letter dated for the end of the school year that explained how they achieved the A. They were to look into the future and report what they specifically did to achieve such a high mark. He found that when they completed this exercise, they in fact actually did what it took to get the A's and reached the highest expectations they had set for themselves. Because they had imagined what it would take to achieve that goal, they had created the recipe for that outcome. Why not give yourself the highest mark possible and move toward that?

Consider writing yourself a letter outlining the change you would like to make in your life and imagine you've already obtained that objective. Identify specific actions to achieve those goals. Give yourself an "A" in your ability to make the change or to reach that goal. Consider how you will feel when you are there.

What is the most courageous thing you've ever done?

How might you use that courage to realize your greatness?

Many people resist doing something really meaningful in their lives. Many do some good things, and some do good things often. But there are many who are reluctant to take the big step that leads them into their "greatness". Greatness doesn't have to be at the same level as Mother Theresa or Mahatma Ghandi, it can be simply stretching out of the comfort zone to achieve more, give more or be more. Here are some examples:

1.) The son of a 72-year-old from Summerland participated in the Ironman competition. As the father celebrated his son's success, he declared his intention to participate in the competition the following year even though he didn't know how to swim. The very next Monday, he started swimming lessons and one year later successfully completed the race. He lived into his greatness.

2.) Two teenage girls from Summerland started their own business selling "Ogopogo Poop" (packaged green jelly beans with an Ogopogo story attached). They didn't just pocket their earnings, but took proceeds to Mexico to deliver books and supplies to help the very underprivileged and seriously challenged "children of the dump". Those girls are living into their greatness.

3.) A woman from Kelowna sold everything she owned and moved lock stock and barrel to Katmandu, Nepal to start an international organization (Intercultural Women's Education Network) buying back young women from slavery and providing them with an education. She lives courageously in crude surroundings, giving back to the world and living into her greatness.

4.) Another woman in Penticton spends one day a week reading to bedridden seniors and claims they give her as much joy as she brings them. She too is living into her greatness.

Sometimes the most meaningful contributions are often simple, selfless acts. What is holding you back from doing one thing that will move you from complacency into the extraordinary? Every act of selflessness helps heal the world.

How many times have you heard someone limit their own potential by stating that they are not University material, or smart enough to reach a goal they would love to attain?

 In fact, when I was in high school, my career counselor suggested I should not even apply for occupational therapy as my grades would not be high enough to qualify. At that time there were 500 applicants for 21 spaces at the University of Alberta. Of course, I am not very good at listening when others tell me what to do and applied anyway. Forty-three years later I would love to be able to tell that teacher about my long and successful career as an occupational therapist!

Michelangelo said "Inside every block of stone or marble dwells a beautiful statue. One needs only to remove the excess material to reveal the art within." What a lovely idea; we can create the possibility of what we are simply by letting ourselves know that it is possible.

When you think about when you were at your happiest in your life, what values were you truly living?

....

....

....

....

....

....

....

....

....

....

....

....

....

....

....

....

....

....

....

....

....

....

....

Where might you be living with a values conflict?

....

....

....

....

....

....

....

....

....

....

....

....

....

....

....

....

....

....

....

....

....

STOP! Think! Discover!

Week 3:

What is Your Life Balance?

*"Be aware of wonder. Live a balanced life,
learn some and think some and draw and paint
and sing and dance and play and work every day some."*
~ Robert Fulghum

H When Anita and I decided to update our **PMS** program, we wanted to make sure that the stories were real. Afterall, we have lived a long time and have many of our own, so why make things up?

I struggled to find a story that felt interesting and current, then realized that at **this** moment I am struggling with life balance as I move out of my active fulltime working life and into a more relaxed way of being.

For years I have worked every spare minute, developing my occupational therapy business, providing services to a large caseload, inventing new ideas for programs and workshops and the multitude of other daily tasks that are required in a busy life. I have been very active and goal oriented for the past forty years. Now my life has more open space and I want to ensure I fill it with meaningful activity. My desire is to continue to feel I make a difference in the lives of others and model how to gracefully move into the life and future I really want. Habitually everyday I start with the same routine of checking work email and then gradually become caught up in the tasks I **think** I need to complete without being mindful of the balance I really want.

I now take time to do the things I have always wanted to do, and yet I find myself continuing to work at tasks that are not a priority for me. So how to truly walk the talk?

I realized that I have not been clear about my intentions for how I really want to live my life. I have no real model for the "retirement" I envision and so struggle to be clear on what I really want on a daily basis. So, after careful consideration I have set clear and realistic goals in terms of how I plan to spend my time. I have clarified my fitness and health goals and I plan to do at least one healthy activity or class every day. I also plan to participate in at least three fun social activities a week. I plan to meditate and journal every day and play my guitar at least five days a week. Making my leisure and health activities a priority allows me to consider how much of my life I want to allocate to work.

*Every week I allocate specific time limits to the various components of my work. It is a "work in progress" but at least it keeps me aware of how many hours I work every day. Instead of eight hours every day I try to limit it to half that time. I remind myself of this intention every morning, just as we talked about in Week 1. We are all in this together; just because we are aware of this process doesn't mean we always **do it** automatically! Now I take a few minutes to consider what I want to accomplish each day which helps me focus on making that a reality.*

In twenty years, I want to be able to look back on how I've spent the hours in this stage of my life and feel satisfied that I eased out of my professional work life while continuing to make a difference in the world. Focusing on my values and intentions allows me to maintain better life balance.

 At 44 years of age I was in a two-year College course when I met Anna, another student my age. She had a keen interest in our studies but never allowed anything to interfere with time with her husband. When there were assignments that required attention after class, or perhaps when a group of us would go for a drink Anna never accompanied us.

Anna and her husband had a long-term loving and close relationship that came first and only. While the rest of the adult students developed close relationships with each other, Anna didn't.

Then tragedy struck. When Anna's husband died suddenly at age 48 she was completely devastated. She had invested in one relationship and only had casual acquaintances outside of her marriage. Although they had what some might regard as a "fairy tale" marriage, she was so out of balance that her life was completely meaningless without her husband. She never recovered and became a sad and lonely young recluse.

What do you think? …

- ❑ How can you relate these stories to your life?
- ❑ What area of your life may need more attention at this time?

"Balance" is a word we use to describe life satisfaction. It's an odd word to describe this characteristic because we all know that when we talk about "balance" in regards to our life it is really nothing like the "weigh scale" definition. We don't all need exactly the same amount of work as play, or exercise and rest time. Balance means something different to everyone. What does "balance" mean to you? If you were living a life of true balance, what would it look like?

Balance from the perspective of living a full and satisfying life can be measured using this Indicator Wheel. It's a tool to help identify areas of your life that you might choose to observe, assess and make changes or adjustments to, then monitor and measure again at a later date.

To use the Indicator Wheel:

Label each segment of the wheel for a specific focus area of your life.

For example: health, spiritual, social, financial, family, education, leisure, intimate relationships, career, or any other area of your life that you would like to focus on.

These should be your personal choices and **not** determined by these examples!

In this sample, the colours represent satisfaction levels in each area. *Some* have high levels of satisfaction, yet several other areas need some attention.

When Hilary used this tool, she **first** focused on the areas of the wheel that were not work related as these were the most important areas for her at that time in her life.

We wonder if Anna would have recovered more quickly from her husband's tragic death if she had invested a bit more time in other areas of her life? The relative importance and the priorities assigned to the different focus areas in one's life is a dynamic, ever-changing situation. Consider **your** life and contemplate where **you** want to focus as you regularly assess your own Indicator Wheel.

External circumstances can knock our life balance out of alignment. Covid19 did this to all of us at the same time. If you are going through an event out of your control, such as the death or illness of someone close to you, a birth, or some other major event, your balance will be impacted. How can you use this wheel to help you regain some semblance of control during changing times?

Your Indicator Wheel

Now it's your turn. Think deeply about this and take your time moving through the process.

It doesn't have to be done in one sitting!

- Label each segment of the wheel for a specific focus area in your life.
- Determine how satisfied you are with your life relative to each segment and indicate your level of satisfaction by appropriately penciling in or colouring the segments.

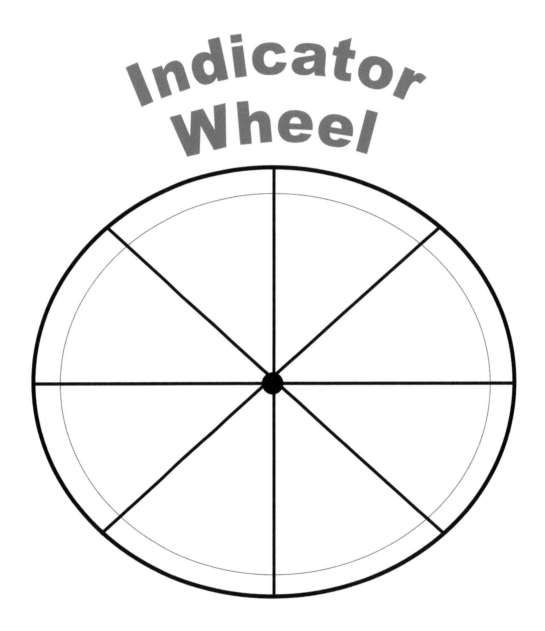

Consider how balanced the wheel is and if are there areas that render the wheel lopsided; thereby compromising its ability to roll along smoothly.

What if you compare your top values to the segments of your wheel? Make a note of the top values you identified in the last module here:

1._____
2._____
3._____
4._____

How do your core values align with the attention you pay to the areas of your wheel?

We can accurately measure the distance to work, the time it takes to walk a mile, how much coffee to put in the coffee maker and the length of our pants. We can measure the longest, the shortest, coldest or hottest, and the time it takes for the earth to rotate, but the measure of the person you are is not so easy! We are often measured by teachers, parents, peers, supervisors and managers, but the methods employed are neither accurate nor useful for the measure of who we are and who we truly want to become.

Consider the ideal balance for your life at this present time, but recognize it may have to be adjusted as circumstances change. Make a schedule on your calendar of what **your** ideal balance would look like. Make a vision board, draw a picture or discover some other creative way to help you clarify your ideal balance.

What will you start measuring? What will you start doing? What will you stop doing? What will you do more of?

What areas of your wheel require some attention?

....

....

....

....

....

....

....

....

....

....

....

....

....

....

....

....

....

....

....

....

....

....

....

Name one thing you can do to tweak an area in your balance wheel that will add to your day to day life...

....

....

....

....

....

....

....

....

....

....

....

....

....

....

....

....

....

....

....

....

....

....

....

....

Week 4:

Treasure Hunts

Treasure hunts are excavations in the landscape of your life! Remember how much fun they were when you were a kid? The idea of a treasure hunt in this program is to help you practice paying attention and to reflect on the area **you choose** to focus on each week. It is up to you to identify what is most important to you…what is the treasure you are hunting for. You can make it as small or as big as you like and can change this to fit your life each week.

You can't fix or change anyone else,
so, you might as well work on yourself!

We all experienced the process of "intellectual learning" in school. It was a means of transferring information from the teacher to the student. It exercised our short-term memory, and we often lost much of the information shortly after the test! Critical thinking skills were not on the agenda. Yet critical thinking skills are exactly what we all need to get through this rapidly changing world. Our habits and conditioning can hinder our progress.

 My sister, Tanya Swaren, developed a two-week learning program that I was privileged to facilitate. It was developed for people in career transition and was designed to assist them in acquiring critical thinking skills and develop their ability to recognize opportunities they were previously unaware of. Many were constrained by mindsets that kept them in jobs they didn't like and stopped them from considering alternative employment when they were unemployed. The success stories that came from that program were too many to mention; but the greatest success was that every participant over the seven-year term of the project gained renewed energy, new options, insights and opportunities. It literally changed lives.

In a world of such rapid and continuous change we need to become enhanced learners. Our world demands more of us now…we need to grow ourselves continuously to meet the changes that affect us every day. We don't have the time or the resources to go to school each time we need to learn something new.

Make this treasure hunt about you and your own interactions, habits, behaviours or interests and don't get sidetracked by the actions of others. Whatever you choose to focus on for the week, simply notice without judgment, but with curiosity and interest. You are always learning more than you think, you just may not be aware of what it is.

Practical Neuroscience

Over the past decade scientists have researched how learning impacts the brain and its development. We all know someone who seems to keep making the same mistakes repeatedly.

It turns out that the brain develops more neuropathways or "roads" for our most common experiences. For example, if the story you tell yourself about your life is that you were bullied as a teenager and your whole life is going to be difficult that is exactly what will happen.

The neuropathways that travel in your brain from the area of decision making to those of emotion will constantly fire the same way unless you consciously change your thoughts. Research has shown that this is possible with reflection and repetition, but it takes time and perseverance. What story are you telling yourself?

What can you change in how you tell your story to ensure it becomes more of what you really want? You can't change what happened in your past but you **can** choose to determine what you learned from it and how you will use that experience in the future.

We can **choose** to say: "I was bullied as a child and it keeps happening to me now. People are bullies".. Or we could **choose** to say "I was bullied as a child and that has made me stronger and more understanding of others who are bullied".

Research has shown that brain development is designed to protect us but our tendency is to focus on undesirable outcomes. For example, if you completed twenty tasks in your day, and nineteen of them went well, which do you think you would focus on? Dr. Rick Hansen, a neuropsychologist and a meditation teacher, suggests in his book, "*The Practical Science of Buddha's Brain*", that we can change the pathways in our brain by changing our focus. Reflection, insight and repetition will eventually physically alter the pathways so the one trail that your brain automatically selects is the one you chose, not the default negative one.

How many of us have experienced this reaction? We are programmed to focus on what didn't go well. For the most part, we should no longer apply that importance to our daily decisions as if we were still living in the dinosaur days. If something didn't go well in that time period, it could mean a life and death experience. Dropping your ice cream cone may have soiled your blouse and you didn't get to eat that tasty treat, but it is not the end of your world!!

If we can learn to focus on the positive experiences in our day, our whole outlook will improve and our brain will reflect that. Dr. Hansen presents a simple exercise to develop a more positive mindset. Choose one of your positive attributes; it can be something as simple as noticing you are friendly, creative or perceptive. Consider the different aspects of this attribute and take a little time to notice that it is a trait that you really have. Notice how this attribute appears in your life and then really *feel* it when you find it. Notice when you have difficulty accepting that this is a part of your personality. If we can focus on the parts of ourselves we like more, we will notice increasing positivity in our lives.

This is your chance to develop the questions that require answers! This is your opportunity to create the learning curriculum that is the most meaningful to you. It will enable you to learn from your day-to-day activities…it's the classroom of your world, the playground of your life!

Your treasure hunt can be about anything you want to develop or enhance, or isolate and change. It's most effective when it is self-identified and self-directed. It may appear as a result of an observation or awareness obtained from the current module, or it could be revealed during your daily routine or the status of your relationships. It can be anything that you want to observe and learn about yourself.

I was a tomboy in a tutu…as a child I was a hellion with my little brother and an angel with my two older sisters. My brother was 100% hellion (although he may not agree now!), so when we got in trouble, (which was often), he made the situation worse by excessive talking while pleading his innocence. My "angel" persona took over for me and I said not a word! Consequently, my brother was often punished while my silence was apparently interpreted as evidence of no fault. I was able to avoid some well-deserved discipline, which I'm not particularly proud of now! One day, when I was 5 years old, I saw the TV show "Candid Camera", and realized that if there were hidden cameras in the trees on my street, the truth would be exposed! It was a life changing moment. I often use that "could be" camera to get a glimpse of another perspective…what does this action look like from there? What might other people see? Is this really the right action or choice? What impact does this have on others?

Treasure hunts will help you become focused and learn more about yourself during your everyday situations and relationships. In general people are proficient at observing others and identifying what they do or don't do well. We all know when others are annoying, irritating and just plain old wrong!

This process requires that you either turn your attention inward or attempt to observe yourself during your interactions within your world. This places the focus on you as opposed to others. It challenges you to choose and commit to one specific learning experience during a normal – or not so normal week and to be hyper-aware of your progress. Why not use that hidden camera to keep an eye on yourself in action and interaction?

This learning habit will take you far beyond the **PMS** Program. If you adopt the "treasure hunt" approach you will become a proficient, intentional learner, more aware and able to develop a greater sense of all you can be throughout your life.

I have found it fascinating that when I am irritated by others it may be an indication that I could exhibit the same behaviour. It isn't pleasant to accept but honest introspection reveals that I can also be irritating to others! I wrote in a previous module about discovering how "triggered" I became when dealing with men who appeared dismissive of women. Another gift from that interaction was my realization that I too can come across as dismissive and overbearing. It has made me reconsider my behaviour at times and really think about how others could be perceiving me. Not always a comfortable place to sit, but definitely a place of growth.

There's more evidence for the importance of treasure hunting; have you ever missed the obvious? If so, you are "normal" according to studies done by Dr. Daniel J. Simons, a psychologist at the University of Illinois. One of Dr. Simons' video studies was featured on 60 Minutes. The video showed two teams of three people (three in white shirts and three in black shirts) intermingled, with each team passing a basketball to only their team members. Viewers were asked to count only the number of passes completed by the team in the white shirts. I counted 15, the "right" answer!

But, there's a catch. The real test was to measure what we were missing while engaged in counting the passes. On a re-play of the same video we saw that while we were busy focusing on counting, a large person in a gorilla suit came into the scene amidst all the activity, theatrically beat his chest and left. We didn't even notice!!!

How is this happening in our lives? What are we missing?

It isn't because we're not observant or that we lack intelligence. In fact, it could be that the more intense or specialized we become, the more likely we are to miss seemingly obvious events and activities. Think about the last time you were in deep thought while driving home, arrived safe and sound but didn't remember the trip? What might you have missed?

How does this impact you at work? It makes sense why so many people, due to the frenetic activity of their workplace, might be oblivious to the ever-present conflict and relationship issues of staff as they walk with purpose and focus from their office to the boardroom. How much of what is being missed is critically important to the decisions being made in that boardroom?

Is there something slipping right past you that could be of great importance? Perhaps you're missing something that could change your opinion or your perspective?

What might you see if you were to occasionally pause and observe what is happening around you? At home, what are you focused on that might distract you from sharing the joy in your child's eyes? What do you need to look up from? You may be walking right past some treasures in your home or organization and don't even know it. How can you look at your life with newborn eyes?

If you are finding you have time and energy to consider treasure hunts while doing **PMS**, we are providing you with some extra ideas to help you grow. As previously mentioned, the **Field Study** module has been added as the last "chapter" to give you more ideas and opportunities to grow. Don't feel obligated to do extra, but if you welcome additional activities there are ideas in that module that will add nourishment to your growth. Each week you can choose an extra treasure hunt, or not! It's up to you.

STOP! You know what to do…breathe, think, reflect and start imagining your new future.

Think hard about what you might chose for your self-directed treasure hunt this week.

....

....

....

....

....

....

....

....

....

....

....

....

....

....

....

....

....

....

....

....

....

....

....

....

....

What might be invisible to you about yourself that you might want to illuminate?

....

....

....

....

....

....

....

....

....

....

....

....

....

....

....

....

....

....

....

....

....

....

....

Week 5:

Shift to the Positive

I can just tell it's going to be a bad day.
I think you should have a more positive attitude.
Okay...I'm positive it's going to be a bad day.

Did your treasure hunt involve something positive about yourself? We hope so, but too often people end up noticing the negatives. We are naturally "fixers" and to fix something, you have to find something wrong with it!

Some people may even be using this **PMS** process to "fix" what's *wrong* in their lives. Who do you know who most easily sees the negative and tends to be immersed in troubles, battles, and other challenging patterns in many areas of their lives?

In contrast, we're hoping you can find someone who seems to see life from a positive perspective and tends to live what appears to be a charmed life. If you look more closely, those "charmed life" people actually do experience problems and challenges. They simply have a positive approach to processing and learning, accepting the good and discarding the negative.

The law of attraction is the theory that our thoughts create our reality. It has been the subject of much discussion, with some embracing the concept and others rejecting it. Regardless of your position, it is an important concept that has encouraged some people to think differently.

If this is true, *what are you thinking...and what are you creating?!* Whether you believe it or not, you can put this theory to the test. Look around and see the evidence for yourself. Some people see the world through a negative lens thinking they must fight to survive. Everywhere they look they see evidence of that negative worldview. Others see the world as a beautiful place and find strong evidence to support their perspective. It's hard to believe that they all inhabit the same planet!

"Every intention sets energy into motion
whether you are conscious of it or not".
~ Gary Zukav

You don't have to look far to find more evidence of people creating their own lives. The friends you choose are a reflection of who you are or will become. Look closely at who you spend your time with. Their actions and behaviours are an example of the templates of your life. It's really quite simple; change your friends and change your life. That is one obvious example of the law of attraction. It's much bigger than that, but it's a start.

There is a story of little boy who loved to wake up on the morning of a big snowfall. He would walk to school, setting the first tracks in the snow and then delight in backtracking on his path. The trail he left in the snow would be a convoluted maze of steps and paths. He would then watch as the other children arrived; they would unfailingly walk in his steps no matter how much they had to go out of their way to do this. They took the path of least resistance as the snow had already been packed down on his trail.

This same principle applies to our brains. Once we have a thought process our brains are more likely to go down that same path (yup, those neuropathways again!). It takes awareness, attention, and effort to change those processes and to create the development of a new "trail". The good news is that we don't have to settle for old patterns. We can create positive new paths; it just starts with a purposeful intention to make that happen. In his book *Social Intelligence*, Daniel Goleman, explains this concept. He talks about the brain's ability to take a new path, but it takes intention and work. If we don't notice that we are going down the same path we can't make a change!!

It all starts with the awareness of your thoughts and thought patterns. What thought patterns are guiding you through your morning rituals? What are you thinking about the people next door or the driver in front of you?

If we all paid attention to the paths we take in our brains and focus on the positive, we could physically change our brains. This concept can also be seen when others compliment you…accept the compliments, let them simmer in your heart and enjoy them.

You may have heard the story of a woman who was moving to a new town and stopped to talk to an elderly man walking with his grandson She asked: "I'd like to move here and want to know what the people are like?" The elderly man replied, "What are the people like where you come from?" The woman responded, "They are miserable, and I can't wait to get away from them". The man answered, "That's what people are like here too" and he walked away holding his grandson's hand. He was soon stopped by a young man who said he was considering this town as a new home for his family and asked what the people are like. Once again, the older man responded with the question "What are they like where you come from?" "They are wonderful people…very friendly and supportive". The elderly man said, "That's exactly what people are like here". There was a question in the little boy's eyes as he heard his grandfather's reply.

Could the grandfather be lying, or how could both of those statements be true?

Developing and using an appreciative approach can create a positive shift in how situations are seen. Appreciative Inquiry or AI is a research theory that moves away from the old problem-solving model toward a more positive growth pattern. Have you noticed if we look for problems that's exactly what we find?! The appreciative approach, based on AI, is a way to focus on **what is working**. Practiced by noticing the best in ourselves, others and the world around us; affirming strengths, successes, and potentials and consciously attaining positive personal growth.

What about when we make that inevitable "mistake"? How do we handle it and how do others respond when we display our imperfections?!

In her book "*Storycatcher*", Christina Baldwin writes about how wrongdoing is managed by the Babemba tribe in southern Africa. She tells of how other activities in the village cease and all community members surround the "offender" to deal with the issue. Each villager recounts everything the person has done right in his life, including good deeds, behaviours and acts of social responsibility. The villagers help "appreciate that person back into the better part of himself" so he is provided the opportunity to remember who he really is and why he is important to the village.

It can be easily forgotten that we are part of a larger system, and what we do can deeply impact others. We don't have to look hard to find examples of how we lean toward discipline and punishment rather than appreciation. In fact, it seems the norm is to ignore the good and only focus on what is wrong! Catching someone doing something right, telling them specifically what it is that you appreciate and why, is a developed skill and can have a positive impact on our relationships.

Recently a manager in a local business was overheard saying to the receptionist, "I know I haven't told you this before, but I really appreciate how you greet people when they come in as if they were a guest in your own home. I think it makes them feel welcome and that makes my job a lot easier. So, thank you for that!" It doesn't take much to imagine how the receptionist felt after receiving that feedback.

Although there is research supporting the positive results of this "appreciative approach", it would be interesting to do your own research…try it yourself! Genuine appreciation can have positive effects on family members, friends and work associates. This can be difficult when annoying behaviours hinder the opportunity to recognize positive behaviour. Challenge yourself to step past those irritations and find something to appreciate. You just might find that the recipient does even more of what you value and less of what irritates you.

Another way to look at shifting to the positive involves a concept called "Hard Time" that has its roots in the prison community. "Hard time" is when individuals fight their jail sentence, focusing on the negative and what isn't working. They tend to be angry and defensive in their interactions with others. You don't need to be in jail to do hard time! How many of us know someone who is almost always negative - someone who on a glorious day will find the one thing that isn't perfect about it. That is the person who is doing "hard time" or viewing the glass as half empty.

But consider Nelson Mandela who chose to live with a positive attitude within the confines of his prison experience and went on to make a positive impact on the world. He chose "easy time" even though he was imprisoned. You can choose "easy time"…even through difficult circumstances, have a positive attitude and appreciate all that comes your way. People who do easy time tend not to worry as much because they know that "this too shall pass" and that in the final analysis worrying doesn't help at all! They have a more relaxed attitude and expect the positive.

Your daily interactions can focus on the positive while retaining a sense of humour. You might try an M.R.I., "Most Respectable Interpretation". An example of this is when someone cuts you off in traffic or is rude to you in a store. The obvious option is to see it as rude or as a personal affront. But what if that person is hurrying to the hospital to see a sick child? None of us know what others are dealing with.

You might be anxious to get to the next week of stories, thoughts and reflections, but hang on! Your time will be better spent going back through any or all the "weeks" up to now, or go to the last module with Treasure Hunts to add to your experience. Interesting how the patterns of our lives drive our behaviours, isn't it?

I usually have a need to get to the end of the current book I'm reading, skimming much of it. This is not that kind of book…and yes, I had to work hard to slow down and reflect, journal and learn at a deeper level. It has been a great exercise for me to pause and reflect, and I'm challenging you to notice your response to the suggestion to do the same.

What stories about yourself are you telling yourself and others? Are these what you want to create more of?

....

....

....

....

....

....

....

....

....

....

....

....

....

....

....

....

....

....

....

....

....

....

....

....

Think of a specific time when you felt most happy, satisfied, fulfilled and valued. What do you most appreciate about yourself in that memory?

....
....
....
....
....
....
....
....
....
....
....
....
....
....
....
....
....
....
....
....
....
....
....

Week 6:

Keeping it Simple

We have too much stuff! We're being told to simplify, downsize, right size, clean our closets and get rid of our junk. "*The Life Changing Magic of Tidying Up*" by Marie Kondo is a great read and shares the wisdom of minimalizing. The YouTube movie "*Minimalism*" by Joshua Fields Milburn and Ryan Nicodemus is compelling and worth the time to watch.

> **"*Too many people spend money they haven't earned,***
> ***to buy things they don't want, to impress people they don't like.*"**
> **Will Rogers**

We don't need to be told that our lives are too complicated, and a big part of it is the accumulation we find ourselves drowning in. If we just stop and think about it, decluttering and simplifying could be just what we need to make some space for living well. It gives us the ability and freedom to have a greater quality of life through activities, family and friends. Come to think about it, wouldn't we much rather be having fun than taking care of "stuff"?

 I read a book called Sidetracked Home Executives, a humourous look at a mother of young children trying to keep up with the living room tent and toy-cluttering life, which was exactly my life at that time! The book came complete with a card system to stay on top of all the minutia of keeping the house clean and tidy in case someone dropped in unexpectedly – possibly the "boss"! I bought it hook, line and sinker. I created this complex card system with daily, weekly and monthly jobs on each colour coded index card, complete with the amount of time to do each job. It worked well, as I distributed some of the cards to my children to do the small jobs on a weekly basis allowing me to keep up the cleaning. When I was telling my aunt about this magical card system to keep spots off the table so I could have more time to play with my kids, she responded with a laugh and said "see this spot?" as she pointed to a stain on her tablecloth. She lifted her coffee cup and planted it firmly on the stain and said "spot's gone…go play with the kids!"

The point is not to *NOT* clean, but rather to have *less stuff* to clean and take care of. Also, to pay attention to how much cleaning is necessary and recognize when it actually becomes a waste of our limited time!

> **'*We go on multiplying our conveniences only to multiply our cares. We***
> ***increase our possessions only to the enlargement of our anxieties.*'**
> **Anna C. Brackett**

We think our stuff is so very valuable. Strange how when we hold a garage sale and put even a nominal price on our treasures, people invariably ask us to reduce the price by half. After all, it's not all that valuable. This is even more apparent when someone dies; usually no one wants the family china or the photograph collection.

In the past three years I have lived through the death of both my parents. We helped them downsize from the family home three times until they eventually moved to a care facility. On each occasion, there were many items that no one wanted. I don't want to leave this kind of mess for my children and so have started the process of getting rid of stuff. In Sweden they call this "death cleaning", but overall, it just makes sense to do this before you aren't able to so you don't saddle your children with the job.

In our community people put their well-used items at the curb so others who might want them can just take them away. The big armchair sat out on the curb for the better part of a week until a neighbor put a price tag on it to suggest it was worth $40. Sure enough, in the morning it was gone! It wasn't valuable, but the price tag suggested it was worth more than it really was, and someone ran off with it!

It's therapeutic to purge; take just one drawer or closet and clear out the unnecessary and unused junk *(yup…that's what it is, so call it what it is)*. There's a beautiful feeling of freedom with each box delivered to the "goodwill", each bag of blankets to the homeless, and the lonely clothes that haven't been worn in years to a consignment or thrift store. Someone else can use and appreciate those items, and let's face it, that is true recycling, re-using and re-purposing. It's kind to our emotional wellbeing and even kinder to the planet.

Some of us believe that if we only had a new car or a bigger house that we would be happy. We strive to make payments on things we can't really afford or impulsively purchase items we don't need simply to keep up with our friends. How happy does that really make us?

Try going to a place where there are no stores and no ability to make purchases. Surround yourself with great friends and people you love. Spend time socializing and doing meaningful activities. Then come back into our consumer driven world and see how important shopping really is.

Every year I go to guitar camp. I park my car in a field and leave it for a week, with no ability or desire to spend money. The sensory overload when I come back out into the "real" world is overwhelming. The urge to stop and shop in those large factory stores is non-existent. The realization of how rich I am with relationships and people I really care about is something I just can't buy.

During Covid-19 it was noticed that people stopped shopping for unnecessary items and due to social isolation were limited in access to the people they cared about. These changes created the realization of what really was important.

How else can we simplify?

Simplifying doesn't only apply to physical possessions.

Are you carrying other people's burdens, worries and "stuff"?

We each carry our own burdens and worries. In coaching we talk about "carrying our own monkeys", a metaphor for our concerns, worries and challenges. Sometimes it is tempting to take on someone else's monkeys, or they might try and give them to us! We can end up with a whole bunch of extra monkeys. We will feel weighted down not only by our own worries but also the worries of others without even realizing we are carrying them.

When we carry other people's monkeys, we may be tempted to play the role of the "hero" which will feed our ego as we attempt to rescue someone else. It may also be an excuse to avoid dealing with our own monkeys because we're so busy with the problems of others! Ultimately though carrying all these extra critters can result in resentments which are not in our best interests and will eventually deplete our energy and diminish our ability to manage our own personal issues.

We may think we do others a favour when we carry their "stuff" for them, but it can limit their ability to grow into their own capacity. We each need to develop the strength it takes to manage the challenges that come our way. What we can do for others is listen, care and let them know they are strong and capable. Caring for others does not mean taking over their burdens. It is more important to look after yourself well and respectfully allowing them to move through their challenges with dignity and moral support. Take responsibility for your own life and let them take responsibility for theirs.

So, whose monkeys are you carrying? Remember: "Not my monkey, not my zoo"!

Try letting go of what you don't need and appreciating what you already have.

You might notice this module it shorter, smaller…*downsized, yay!*

Get out of the clutter and enjoy
your freedom!

What possessions are holding you hostage?

....

....

....

....

....

....

....

....

....

....

....

....

....

....

....

....

....

....

....

....

....

....

....

....

....

What names can you give to the monkeys you're carrying?

....

....

....

....

....

....

....

....

....

....

....

....

....

....

....

....

....

....

....

....

....

....

....

....

....

Week 7:
Differing Personality Gifts

All different…all beautiful!

Too often we jump to judgment when others demonstrate their differences, which limits our relationships and creates more conflict that complicates our lives.

There are many tools available to help us better understand ourselves and others. One we use in our coaching practices is the MBTI (Myers Briggs Type Inventory). It has it's roots in Jungian theory, is supported with over 50 years of research and continues to demonstrate reliability and validity.

We have found the MBTI to be helpful for people to recognize and understand their own preferences and those of others which may differ significantly from their own. If used properly, it helps people appreciate rather than judge differences, and to complement rather than divide. This module is not meant to be a complete description of the MBTI. For a more complete understanding we recommend reviewing it on-line, taking a course or having the inventory administered by a qualified professional to really understand it.

Isabel Briggs Myers noted that *"…the theory is that much seemingly chance variation in human behaviour is not due to chance; it is in fact the logical result of a few basic, observable differences in mental functioning."*

Our "type preferences" guide our most natural choices and how we interact in the world. To demonstrate this, try this exercise…pick up a pen or pencil with your **non-dominant hand** and write your name.
  • What did you notice?
  • What words would you use to describe the effort/experience?
  • How does your signature look – what is the outcome?

Now change hands and write your name with your dominant hand.
  • How does it compare to the first effort?
  • What is the outcome?

This exercise demonstrates what we refer to as a *preference*. It is possible to write your name with your non-dominant hand, but most of us find it easier, as well as more natural and efficient to use our dominant hand. The MBTI helps identify other preferences that may be less obvious than "handedness". Imagine working for a long period of time in a job that is "out of preference".

People often select work based on monetary incentives and may not realize that their exhaustion and unhappiness is due to being constantly immersed in an "out of preference" role.

If you have ever injured your dominant hand, you'll understand the degree of difficulty involved in living "out of preference" for a period of time.

Some may worry that these types of assessments "pigeon hole" and limit individuality and that could happen when they are used inappropriately. But there are many benefits to gaining insights to our own and others' personalities. We maintain that this process should open us to greater possibilities and strengthened relationships. Knowing and understanding your preferences could help you have a greater understanding of yourself, love who you naturally are and let go of the comparisons to others that diminish your personal power.

The four MBTI dichotomies are:

- **Extraversion - Introversion:** the way you naturally prefer to obtain and direct energy
- **Sensing – Intuition:** how you naturally gather information
- **Thinking – Feeling:** the way you most naturally make decisions
- **Judging – Perceiving:** how you organize yourself in your external world

The best way to help illustrate how these differences impact our lives is to relate stories of how it has influenced our relationships!

Both Anita and I are extroverts. We love talking things through and being actively involved with others. We find it energizing to discuss issues and may alter our opinions during the conversation as we hear what we are saying. We come up with ideas we had not considered prior to hearing ourselves talk. This can be very disconcerting for our more introverted family members who may not say much at all. When my husband has an opinion, I know that he has thought about it deeply before he has said anything to me. He loves to have alone time and too much company overwhelms him.

Extroverts get energized by being with others and introverts prefer to recharge by being alone.

Sensing – Intuition: How you gather information

When buying a car, my husband would review consumer reports, gather information from multiple car dealers and check with everyone he knew. It nearly drove me crazy because I wanted to just try a few models and buy the one I liked. After many years, he didn't even mention that he was researching a good car until he found the top three. Only then would he take me for the test drives. What I realized and finally acknowledged much later, is that the reason we successfully purchased good cars over the years is that it took the preferences of both to make the best decision.

How do you take in information? Do you see the facts and the specific details or do you see the possibilities of what could occur?

Thinking-Feeling: How you make decisions

In my role as a coach and mentor in a growing occupational therapy practice, I work with a number of different therapists with different styles. I notice that the therapists who make decisions from a "thinking" preference often better manage the related stressors of the job as they can move naturally to a more objective approach to their work. Those therapists with a "feeling" preference tend to empathize with their clients and actually can take on those emotions themselves. They have more difficulty maintaining their boundaries and consequently can become more stressed. I also notice that they appear to find it easier to form emotional bonds with their clients resulting in better rapport. Both approaches in relating to others have advantages and disadvantages; being aware of how you make decisions can result in a better understanding of this process.

Logic has been the measure of success for centuries. Many aspired to higher levels of logic which has been equated to their intelligence and success. We now know that other factors need to be considered when measuring intelligence, fulfillment, satisfaction and success.

As with anything your first priority is to become aware of yourself and your automatic responses. It's important to be objective in examining how the current results are working for you before you can assess, evaluate, develop or change your thinking. So, the challenge is on.

Do you make major decisions based on how you feel about an issue? Or is your decision based on a careful and objective analysis of the facts?

Judging-Perceiving – How we orient ourselves in the world

Hilary, with a "Judging preference" (not judgmental!) is somewhat a creature of habit. She values routines and likes to follow a well-planned schedule. She prefers to have few changes to her schedule, is organized and almost always on time. She sets goals and systematically works her way through them. Hilary likes to complete tasks and is greatly satisfied by her completed to-do list at the end of her week. The only way she enjoys being spontaneous is if she's had time to plan it!

Anita, with a "Perceiving preference", chooses to "go with the flow". She likes variety in her work and social activities. She loves spontaneity and is open to change. She is comfortable "flying by the seat of her pants", welcomes unexpected twists and loves to just let life happen. She manages her work schedule and has the ability to plan and organize but it is not written in stone.

When we first worked together facilitating a workshop, these differences could have had a negative impact on our relationship. Fortunately, with the MBTI understanding, we had the ability to acknowledge and value these differences. It could have been irritating, but we were able to see the humour as we struggled with each other's approach! It turned out to be a great experience, a fun memory and a good story to tell.

When we work together, we complement each other's strengths with Hilary providing more organization and Anita insisting that there is wiggle room in the schedule. Rather than getting frustrated and upset with her, Hilary loves nothing better than teasing Anita about her "**P**-ness"!

The Myers Briggs Personality Inventory is one of many assessments that can help you understand your own preferences, recognize the differences between you and other people and gain insight into how to bridge that gap. This understanding can help you accept the other person's needs and contributions.

It's natural to be different

Each personality type naturally guides career choices, relationships, communication and learning styles, to name just a few areas impacted. These preferences exist beneath our actions, habits and behaviours. They are worthy of our awareness and exploration to better understand how they influence our lives.

Keep in mind how difficult it was to write your name with your non-dominant hand. Now imagine how exhausting it might be for an extrovert with a sensing preference to have a job working alone as an accountant or an introvert to have a career in marketing that requires constant interaction with large groups of people.

It's important to remember we are all different and can be more effective when we understand and respect our differences. Simply noting that we are not all the same is a huge step. We might naturally measure others according to our own style and preference. At times we might assume others think the same way we do and may be surprised when someone reacts differently than we anticipate. Respecting and honouring these differences can bring fresh perspectives and insights. Sometimes we make assumptions about those closest to us because we think they should behave more like we do! We may assume family members share traits and should therefore understand each other better. Have a look at your family of origin to see if you can identify differing preferences – it's natural to be different!

When I initially took personality assessments the results never seemed to fit. Many years later, I realized that I had been answering the questions the way my family of origin would have valued. I was naturally and spontaneously different in our family of six, and when I finally realized what I was doing and answered the way I truly felt, the results fit like a comfortable pair of shoes. I was able to stop measuring myself against them….in my view, I always fell short. Now I can love and appreciate them and honour myself and our differences.

You can practice noticing differences in your family and your co-workers by paying attention to the amount of information people need, how it might be presented, how they make decisions and how they do the work that needs to be done. Are they able to work on a team or do they prefer working alone? An even better focus is to see yourself in action…how are your preferences perceived and how might they affect others? How might others see **you**…and how might you impact their lives? You can't change anyone else, but you can understand your impact on others, and you can notice and respect similarities, differences, and natural preferences. You can have both the choice and the ability to enhance your skills and capacity within your own natural preferences. Stretch your awareness as you allow others to be who they most naturally are.

Regardless of your preferences you can develop alternatives with awareness and effort. If you live in a more creative world you might need to stretch your logic for a more balanced whole brain experience. Exercising your brain is as important as a workout for your body.

Just when you think you understand this, something interesting happens. Apparently, as we age there is a shift. You might be surprised to discover that around 60 you'll find yourself naturally leaning toward and developing the less preferred dichotomies that were your lifelong subconscious choices!

What do you notice about your natural tendencies? Are you a planner or more spontaneous?

Do you make decisions because they feel right or because they are logical?

....

....

....

....

....

....

....

....

....

....

....

....

....

....

....

....

....

....

....

....

....

....

Do you get energized by a quiet evening at home or by a lively social activity?

Are you a details person or do you see the bigger picture and all the possibilities that could occur in a situation?

....

....

....

....

....

....

....

....

....

....

....

....

....

....

....

....

....

....

....

....

....

Stop for CPR!
Consider - Ponder - Reflect!

Week 8:

Sensory Intelligence

In the last module we talked about the different personality preferences and how they impact our relationships and our lives. Another area that impacts how we get along in our environments and with others is Sensory Intelligence.

Sensory intelligence is defined as having the insight and awareness of the primitive sensory wiring of our brains and understanding the effect this has on everyday living. When we interpret and interact with the world, we filter sensory input through the senses. We see, hear, smell, taste, touch and move and then respond accordingly. Dr. Annemarie Lombard is an occupational therapist who researched and wrote the book *"Sensory Intelligence"* which details how this factor impacts our lives and our relationships. It provides information to help us understand and reflect on our own sensory processing systems and appreciate how others may process and respond differently.

Consider this:

- *Does clutter in your environment irritate you?*
- *Do you have difficulty concentrating when there is a radio playing in the background?*
- *Do different textures or flavours of food bother you?*
- *Are you aware of the labels and seams on clothing?*
- *Do you get nauseated when travelling in a vehicle?*

These are a few things to consider about sensory processing. Dr. Lombard's book provides a lot of useful and enlightening information including how to identify your sensory preferences and manage sensory thresholds more effectively.

Defensive Sensory System:

- Low sensory threshold
- Sensitive to stimuli
- Small levels of sensory input create tension, anxiety, avoidance and anger
- Difficult to *limit* stimulation

Seeking Sensory System:

- Seeks out sensory input
- Manages easily in high levels of high sensory input
- Easy to *seek out* stimulation

Google Dr. Lombard and Sensory Intelligence for more information about it.

Neurological regulation refers to how much information the brain requires to stimulate the nervous system. When the brain responds to sensory information, it sensitizes to it and recruits more brain cells to respond. When it becomes familiarized, it stops noticing and transmitting messages about that input. This balance is what helps us stay focused and allows us to effectively process sensory information. People have varying levels of neurological regulation at different times, depending on a number of factors including emotional status and arousal level.

Sensory Tree Model

Imagine a tree with leaves, branches and deep roots. **Sensory Avoiders** (those who do not like much sensory stimulation) are like the roots of a tree. They prefer a quiet, darker place with little sensory input. They provide the grounding and structure for the rest of the tree to grow.

Sensory Seekers are the leaves of the tree. They are constantly moving in the wind, reaching for new sensations and experiences. They welcome and enjoy activity, variety, and change.

The trunk of the tree represents people with "**typical thresholds**" that are neither high nor low. They describe themselves as easy going and tend to be able to get along with both sensory seekers and sensory avoiders. They are the glue that hold organizations, societies, and families together.

Low registers are like the low branches of the tree. They can be dreamers, and yet easily perform the tasks required of them without experiencing sensory disruption. They are acutely aware of their sensory environment but do not tend to over respond.

Sensory sensitives are like the surface roots of the tree. They are inclined to be more tolerant of busy environments but also prefer quietness, peace and calm in their day, even though they may not actively seek that out.

Sensory Processing impacts our ability to learn; if we are at an ideal level of sensory stimulation, we can absorb new information. If we are under stimulated, we may be sleepy, and if we are over-stimulated, we may be anxious. In both situations learning is difficult.

Sensory Processing also impacts our ability to look after ourselves.

 Earlier in my life, I was in an unhappy marriage, dealing with developing a new career and building a house. We moved into our house while it was unfinished, and I no longer had a stable foundation in my home due to the constant disruptions. One day I found myself sitting in the closet with the door closed. I have never really understood until I learned about sensory intelligence that what I was doing was limiting the sensory input I was receiving to allow my frayed emotional system some down time.

When my son was a teenager and going through all the angst that stage in life involves, we used to talk while walking. The movement and the deep pressure involved in walking would calm us both down so we could manage the difficult conversations. Neither of us knew why this worked better than sitting and talking, but we knew it helped us get through those tough times, so we kept doing it. Now I understand how it calmed our firing emotions in those turbulent days.

 Being self-employed for most of my life and a multi-tasker by necessity and preference, I drove those close to me crazy with my extreme level of activity! Also, naturally social and hyperactive, it was unusual that I loved the weekly five-hour solitary drive to Vancouver. Family and friends would suggest audio books to keep me entertained on the road, but surprisingly, I enjoyed the quiet time with no radio. They sometimes expressed concern for my solitary drive and at times wanted to keep me company and ride with me.

The extrovert in me was mystified as to why I would prefer to be alone. But learning about sensory intelligence has made this so much more understandable. We are human beings and looking at ourselves through only one lens, one model, or one philosophy does not paint the whole picture! The blend of understanding myself through both MBTI and Sensory Intelligence in this situation makes so much more sense.

So how can Sensory Intelligence help with self care? Understanding our preferences and the ability to manage input in different sensory areas creates a greater awareness to determine when things are getting out of control, or alternatively when we need to get moving.

Specifically, it could help to:

- Put something in your mouth - it doesn't have to be food, but the action of drinking, sucking or eating is calming. This could be a reason many of us eat to self soothe!
- Move your body - get up from whatever you are doing and do something different.
- Touch something that has a texture; if you need calming; touch a soft item, if you need stimulation touch something cold or rough.
- Look at something - if you need calming close your eyes; if you need stimulating then look at a busy scene or something colourful.
- Listen - music can either calm or stimulate you. Pay attention to what you need.

Take the time to notice where you are in your sensory processing. If needed, take the time to self regulate; you decide how long that time needs to be depending on your level of arousal.

Dr. Lombard suggests "Taking 5". Take a break, make a change or just notice what is going on in your sensory levels. It could be:

- *Just five seconds* - close your eyes and take a couple of deep breaths
- *Or five minutes* - get up and move, go to the bathroom, get a drink of water
- *Five hours* - do something pleasurable for a day, go to a concert
- *Five days* - take a break from work over a long weekend and change your environment
- *Or five weeks* - take a long holiday and get away!
- *And so on....*

Take the time to notice how your senses process different stimuli and what calms or stimulates you. This will help you to determine whether to calm down or access more sensory input. Insight and knowledge of the sensory processing system are powerful tools for self care.

What is one thing you notice about your ability to handle sensory input?

What is one self-care strategy you could apply to help you become more aware of your sensory stressors?

Possibility Mind Shift

Week 9:

Relationships

The most beautiful discovery true friends make
is that they can grow separately without growing apart.
~ Elisabeth Foley

We all have many different relationships in our lives. They ebb and flow, becoming more important to us at different times. Sometimes they fade away.

When you consider the timeline of your life and the relationships you have experienced, look back and think about the similarities and patterns in those relationships.

One of the most fundamental relationships is the one we have with our parents. We are born into a family forming its own patterns and interactions. The different personalities and histories of the parents blend into their own unique mosaic. We are catapulted into this picture and learn how to survive and hopefully thrive within it. Some of us are luckier than others and have the experience of warm and loving parents. Some aren't so fortunate and have to deal with unhealthy or non-nurturing relationships. But we get what we get and we have to move forward. We can choose to take the good and learn from the not so good.

We move from our family of origin to discover our own personality and style. We do this through experiencing others as a child, then as a teenager and as an adult. These were times when you were formulating your own interpersonal style.

Some might define those relationships as intense and changing; others would say they were comfortable and stable. We cycled through those earlier times learning what was important and practicing how to interact with others.

Factors that contribute to who and how our relationships are defined include the people around us, our role models and the leaders who shaped our expectations of what it is like to be in relationship. The most intimate relationship you will ever have is with yourself.

Consider how many people go through their whole lives not feeling good about who they are. In our coaching practices we often meet people who are challenged by not valuing themselves. The most intelligent and talented person can feel they contribute little to the world when they don't fully appreciate the gifts they offer. That feeling of not liking yourself can affect everything in your life. It can make you feel unlovable and unworthy. It can cause you to sabotage your own goals or feel unsatisfied in many situations.

Studies have shown that self-compassion has many benefits including reducing self-criticism, reducing stress hormones such as cortisol, and healing from the perceived lack of love in childhood. A strategy to help with feeling more compassionate towards yourself is to think of someone who really loves you. It can be anyone, even a pet! Imagine that person or pet is with you, showing you how much they love you in their gestures, facial expression and voice. Allow yourself to receive the love and caring they offer. The experience of receiving care primes the pathways of your brain to allow you to be more compassionate towards yourself.

Low self-esteem is often made worse by our internal critic, or what we call the duck! The duck is that inner voice quacking "that was a dumb thing to say" or "you'll never amount to anything." This self-talk builds the negative pathways in your brain. We say *"shut the duck up!"* But before you shut it up, be aware of the internal critic, re-evaluate and modify the messages to create a shift in how you feel about yourself.

Those who live according to their values have better self-esteem compared to those who don't! Interesting how it all ties back to some basic, fundamental ideas.

When you look back at your Wheel of Life exercise, are you satisfied with the segment that evaluates relationships? What is your vision of the relationship(s) you really want and deserve?

If you know what you want, you have a better chance of getting it, as successful outcomes rely on a clear vision.

We can all learn from Johnny, a young man with Down Syndrome.

As a packer in a supermarket, Johnny didn't feel he was very important or "smart" enough. But he really wanted to make a difference to the people he served every day. He gave a lot of thought to it and decided he would share one of his favourite "Thoughts of the Day" with them by putting it onto paper and into their grocery bags.

Every day when he went home from work, he considered another message he thought was important. He enlisted his father's help with putting his thoughts onto the computer, cutting them into separate messages and signing the back of each one. At work, as he packed each customer's bag, he would include his personally signed "Thought for the Day". Time went by and one day the manager of the store noticed the lineup for Johnny's till was far longer than the others. He opened other cashier stations and asked people to move to them, but everyone wanted to be in Johnny's line. They loved getting their "Thought of the Day" from him and preferred to wait.

Soon the other workers in the store also started making a greater effort to make the store a place that customers would feel valued and recognized. The business was booming as customers enjoyed shopping in a store where they felt valued and special. This story is from a movie by Ken Blanchard and Barbara Glanz.

Often it is the simplest things we do that make the greatest difference. Have you ever been told about something you did that made a difference to another person? Perhaps it was something you did without thinking and likely didn't even consider it until you were reminded.

What small action can you take to make a difference in the lives of those around you?

Intimate relationships can be puzzling and complex as the "Hollywood" stereotypes fashion our expectations. What we see every day is far from the templates that have influenced us. We may be miserable if we desire something that only exists on the silver screen or in the neighbours home when they are on their best behaviour!

Sometimes we don't even realize who we are being...

Katherine, a mature woman attending one of our workshops, arrived wearing her "expert hat" and her "corporate suit of armor". During her introduction she was quick to describe her level of importance through her title, degrees and accomplishments, and seemed ready to diminish others as well as the workshop offerings.

It was apparent she had put up a wall with the potential to negatively affect the other participants as well as the learning process. The morning of the second day of the workshop Katherine apologized to the group. Apparently, after reflecting on how others had demonstrated their authenticity the evening before, she courageously confessed to wearing her "mask".

Katherine expressed the degree of difficulty she had in showing her genuine self, but in this safe environment she came to a profound realization. She tearfully acknowledged how difficult it was for her to step out of her credentials and expertise and just be herself. It was only then we started to see and appreciate the talented and beautiful woman she was. The difference in her over the next two days was remarkable. Her face became more youthful as she discovered how much more the other participants responded to her with open hearts when she revealed her true self. She says she still struggles to take the mask off but now knows how it prevents her from connecting with others in a more meaningful way.

Our environment, profession, roles or habits can become barriers to being our "whole" and real selves. It's nearly impossible to see ourselves in action; to notice those qualities that may be limiting our relationships. Knowing who you really are and becoming aware of the "masks" and "suits" we wear can help us experience the refreshing freedom of being truly authentic.

Try this exercise: Take a blank sheet of paper to make your own mask. Create the picture or words that others see on the outside of the mask. Then draw or describe what you are not allowing others to see about you on the inside of the mask.

We all wear masks when we don't feel safe in relationship. What do you need to feel safe with the people you care about? And what do "they" need to feel safe in a relationship with you?

 Since I was a teenager I've always worn make-up…every day. Even when I had three young children. I would wake up early every morning and applied my eyes and lips while I sipped my morning coffee. I'm convinced that even my children wouldn't have recognized me without my makeup should they have passed me on the street!

But when my sister, Tanya and I joined the gym in the downtown building where our office was, we had to be up at 5 am to start our day. I finally bypassed the makeup. We showered at the gym after the workout and then headed straight to the office. After the first week I asked Tanya if she noticed that people at the gym seemed unfriendly, a little stuck up? Her surprise was evident when she replied that the people were interesting and wonderful. Bam!!! There it was. I instantly knew from that comment that it was not other people who were unfriendly or stuck up, but ME who was not even giving eye contact or connecting with others! The very next day, I started engaging in conversations…with the interesting and fun people at the gym. And to my surprise, I didn't scare even one of them without my makeup…that I know of!

How do you show the people in your life that you care for them? What has to happen in your relationships for you to feel appreciated and loved?

> **Piglet sidled up to Pooh from behind.**
> **"Pooh!" he whispered. "Yes, Piglet?"**
> **"Nothing," said Piglet, taking Pooh's paw.**
> **"I just wanted to be sure of you."**
> ~ *A.A. Milne*

In his book *"The Five Love Languages"* Gary Chapman describes the various ways people demonstrate love. He talks about the importance of learning your own primary love language; the way you feel appreciated. It's important to consider how your "love language" may vary from that of the important people in your life. If you demonstrate love by doing things for others or expressing your appreciation for them but they feel more valued or loved when you give them tangible gifts, there is a gap. Once you identify your preferred love language and understand others may have a different preference, you can communicate more effectively by doing what matters most to the significant people in your life.

 My mother showed her family that she loved them by buying presents. When her children were ill, she would show her concern by bringing us a little gift that she knew we would like. She really appreciated receiving gifts too, no matter how small, as it made her feel special. She spent hours picking out items that would be cherished by the receiver, knowing that it was a way that she could show how much she cared. My husband, on the other hand, shows his appreciation by doing things for the people he cares about. He goes over to his elderly mother's home and mows the lawn. He does chores for others often leaving without even talking to them at all. To him, "service" is his gift of choice!

Creating a vision for your relationships gives you a blueprint for what you really want them to look like. Start with the relationship that is the most important to you. This may be a life partner, a parent, a child or a close friend. Choose a person you have a relationship with that is important to you in some way at this point in your life. Take some time to reflect on just that one relationship.

But don't worry, we won't stop there. In the next module you will evaluate all the important relationships in your life and what you'd like them to grow into.

What makes you feel valued in your relationships?

....

....

....

....

....

....

....

....

....

....

....

....

....

....

....

....

....

....

....

....

....

....

....

....

What one thing might you do to make a positive impact on that special relationship?

....

....

....

....

....

....

....

....

....

....

....

....

....

....

....

....

....

....

....

....

....

....

....

STOP!!

Week 10:

Wherever You Go,
There You Are!

In the middle of all our relationships, here we are! When we think about all the relationships in our lives, it's interesting to consider how each one impacts us. Some bring positive feelings and energy; others just don't feel quite right or they seem to drain our reserves. Some are so much more important, involve more time, and require more investment than others. Our relationships change over time; are they changing the way we want them to or do we allow them to randomly morph into our future? You are at the centre of these changes, and you can influence how you impact those relationships that make up your world.

Do you have people in your life that drain your energy? Do they make you so tired that you can only spend limited time with them? How about those that nurture and support you? These people are easy to spend time with as you both leave each interaction energized and feeling good.

Over our lifetimes we will have friends that remain special to us for decades and others who come and go. It seems some are in our lives for specific periods of time and fill a need. An example would be as a young parent the friends you make with those who have similar aged children. You may not have chosen to spend a lot of time with these people under other circumstances, but you have something in common. As your children grow and move on, these friendships change and may no longer fit into the next stages of your life.

In all these relationships, there is one constant…YOU! Consider *who you are* in your relationships. You might be the supporter, with a listening ear and a helping hand, happy to be behind the scenes. You may be the one who shakes things up by asking questions or inviting change and driving activity. Or you could be described as solid and responsible, ensuring strength and continuity.

> ➢ How might you describe yourself in relationship with others?
> ➢ What do you think it might be like for others to be in a long-term relationship with you?
> ➢ Who do YOU want to be in that relationship?

Family, work, community…they all bring similar relationship rewards and challenges. We may invest more time and attention in family and close friends yet forget that work relationships may be the ones costing us the most in terms of emotions, time and energy.

Are you the same person with your family as you are at work? Are your actions with others congruent with your core values? Check back with "Week 2" to see how those values impact your relationships. Giving yourself and your relationships, the benefit of intention, respect and clarity brings great rewards.

Sometimes attitude, gratitude and contribution make the difference.

You have evolved in the last ten weeks since starting on this **PMS** journey…how has that impacted others in your orbit?

We have all had the experience of having people in our lives that are negative and draining. Are these relationships that you want in your life or are they actually unwanted monkeys?! At times we may to choose to move beyond these relationships if they are absorbing too much of our time and energy or are having a negative effect on us. This can be a difficult decision especially if they rely on you for support. However, it is important to recognize you may be enabling them in their negative and energy draining behaviour. Setting boundaries with an honest and caring conversation may help manage the energy drain in a relationship. If you are obligated to spend time with them simply limiting the contact may help you manage more effectively.

There may be times when we look at our partner or a friend and wonder who they are? We may wonder why we're sitting across the table from a person we don't even like and appears to possess few redeeming qualities. That attitude or perspective, over time, will jeopardize and likely terminate the relationship.

I noticed at times I couldn't seem to find anything I really loved about my partner. The faults I noticed seemed to glare at me and I was having difficulty seeing past them. Alone in my car one day I realized I had been viewing him from a negative mindset, only noticing the things I didn't like. I made a conscious choice to change my perspective, focusing on his positive attributes. He has a lot of positive qualities and once I started paying attention to them, I became more loving and I started enjoying the time we had together again. Sometimes I have to kick myself to remain positive and remember to have this appreciative approach.

**We need old friends to help us grow old
and new friends to help us stay young.**

Take some time to evaluate your relationships. Consider those that are most important to you. Jot down a number between 1 – 10 (10 being highest) beside each one to indicate their level of importance in your life, and a second number between 1 – 10 (same scale!) to identify your level of satisfaction in that relationship.

- Primary (or intimate) Relationship
- Child/Children
- Parents
- Siblings
- Friends
- Coworkers

Identify one thing you can let go of or that you can invest in each of these relationships?

Notice any patterns? What is your role in those patterns?
Where do you need to give more attention and energy?

The purpose of this exercise is to help laser down to the most important actions in your most significant relationships…the ones that are going to have the most impact on your life. Be specific in what you choose to focus on and make your goals manageable and realistic.

Do you have difficulty letting go of feelings, judgments and situations? There are times when it's better to just let it go and give up the heaviness of control.

> There is a story of two Zen monks walking along a muddy country road. They came upon a young woman who was trying to cross the road. She was wearing a beautiful kimono that would have been ruined by the mud. The older monk picked her up and carried her to the other side of the road, set her down and she went on her way. The monks continued on their journey and many hours later the younger one asked "Why did you carry the girl across the road when you know monks are not supposed to touch a woman?" The elder replied "I put the girl down hours ago, why are you still carrying her?"

What are you still carrying that you need to put down?

Imagined slights, long ago arguments, past shames, failed relationships and resentments can all accumulate on our shoulders and weigh us down. Holding on to them depletes energy and carves away at our ability to enjoy our lives. Can you identify where you carry that emotional load? Take a moment and consider where you feel the tension in your body. Could that weight you are carrying be a past shame or resentment? It may show up as a burden on your shoulders straining your neck muscles. Could it be that you are carrying other people's problems? Some of the tension can be from too many hours in front of a computer, but how much of it might be an emotional load?

There is a high price to pay for not letting go of past resentments and unfortunate circumstances. But being aware of these emotions is a prerequisite to consciously letting them go and moving forward in a positive manner.

Some of this negative energy can come from self-inflicted comparison and judgment. Have you ever been in a situation where you felt threatened by someone else's looks or talents? Do you ever compare yourself to others and come up feeling "less than"?

 I learned a valuable lesson from a woman I knew in University and later worked with. Katrine is a wise and accomplished woman who enjoys the company of others. She told me about working with a young woman who was not only talented but exceptionally beautiful. Katrine tried to avoid her because she continually felt that she didn't measure up. She confided in a close friend to deal with the "Green Eyed Monster".

The friend asked her if she had ever admired a piece of art. "Of course," she responded! "Well would you feel inadequate when in the presence of that piece of art and avoid looking at it?" "Of course not" she responded indicating she would never compare herself to a piece of art. "Well what would happen if you behaved the same way in the presence of this beautiful young woman. What would happen if you enjoyed her beauty without comparing yourself to her? Could you then be in her presence and not feel inadequate?" asked the friend. Katrine thought long and hard about this and realized she was depriving herself of being in the presence of beauty. She came to enjoy this young woman and soon appreciated her for more than just her physical attributes.

We all have strengths and abilities to make unique contributions. Recognize yours so you can acknowledge and enjoy them while allowing yourself to freely appreciate the unique qualities of others as well! What would the world be like if we could rejoice in the abilities of each other without feeling threatened and less than the other?

What would happen if your intention was to stop comparing yourself to others?

When you get up in the morning do you consider your intentions for the day? Imagine waking with an energizing stretch and a thoughtful moment. Your intention might be to show appreciation or gratitude to all those you encounter, or to elicit a smile from as many people as possible, or perhaps to listen more for greater understanding. Your intention might be to slow down and enjoy even the mundane activities, or to reconnect with your sense of humour and find the funny in even the most frustrating! Just imagine how creating a focus of intention might influence your interactions at the grocery store or your day at work. How might your day be more enjoyable if you approached it with intention?

 During the Covid 19 quarantine I found making an intention for each day. It improved my productivity and allowed me to see the progress I was making during the time I had to socially isolate. This daily routine helped me to manage the quarantine more effectively and allowed me to feel more productive.

What is getting in the way of being aware and what would help you clarify your own intentions every day?

Because, after all, wherever you go, there you are...
So, make it good!

What roles do you take on in the different relationships in your life?

....

....

....

....

....

....

....

....

....

....

....

....

....

....

....

....

....

....

....

....

....

....

....

....

Focus on one of the relationships you have listed and really notice as much as you can about it.

....

....

....

....

....

....

....

....

....

....

....

....

....

....

....

....

....

....

....

....

....

....

....

....

....

STOP!!!

Week 11:
Communication 101

"For it wasn't into my ear you whispered,
but into my heart."
~ Katie Tegtmeyer

From a coaching perspective *(and life in general)* the importance of listening can never be overestimated. Before we jump into the awareness of how we talk or deliver our message, take some time to increase your awareness about your skill level as a listener. Good listeners will pass the test on hearing content. But what about listening for more, *with more than your ears*?

In her book *"Storycatcher"*, author Christina Baldwin suggests that we listen with the "ear" in our h**ear**t. What benefits do you think you might gain from increasing your ability to not just listen, but to really **hear?** …It's a whole-body experience!

Here's a challenge. Try listening differently - for more than just content. Listen for:

❑ Feelings…*what is that person feeling in the message?*

❑ What isn't being said…*what else is under the message?*

❑ Beliefs…*what beliefs might drive the message?*

❑ *And finally, for content! You already do this!*

Equally important is the ability to speak clearly and with authenticity.

In her book, *"Fierce Conversations"* Susan Scott talks about having real conversations about things that matter most with the people you care about. The author suggests that too often we postpone important conversations; we put off talking to our teenagers about sex and drugs in the hope that if we don't bring it up it will go away. Sometimes we don't talk about our concerns because of the risk involved, so important things get left unsaid. It is an awkward silence that gives birth to "the elephant in the room"; it then grows between us. Some of the things often left unsaid might be the words and feelings that articulate the importance of our relationships. We talk about content but may forget to say how much we appreciate the other for their patience, support, objective opinion or simply for just being there…for their friendship or concern.

Our lives, relationships and work succeed or fail one conversation at a time. We need to listen and engage in each conversation as if it is the last one we will have with this person. It could be! None of us know what the future will hold. What are you not saying to the people who matter most? What is it you really want or need to say?

Become aware of your part in conversations. Notice when you avoid the topic, change the subject, hold back or tell little "white lies" in your attempt to move to a safer subject. Take an opportunity at least once a day to stop, take a deep breath and then step forward courageously and respectfully to say what you really believe. Say something that's true for you, that supports both you and the other person in the relationship and watch the results.

> ***"Sticks and stones may break our bones,***
> ***but words will break our hearts."***
> *~ Robert Fulghum ~*

Sometimes it's not *what* we say, but <u>how</u> we say it that becomes the communication challenge. Dr. Eric Berne's theory of **Transactional Analysis** gives us an interesting tool that we like to use to examine communication interactions. This theory suggests that we all have "alter egos": parent, adult and child. Through habit and conditioning we communicate and interact from one of these alter egos. The challenge is to recognize which of the ego states you occupy at the time and to notice if it is appropriate for the relationship or circumstance. Based on Dr. Bernes theory we have modified the Parent, Adult and Child alter egos to "Big, Equal and Small" egos. We call it the BS Communication Model!

The following represents the "alter-ego states" we communicate from:

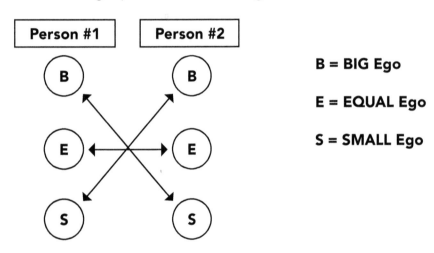

B = BIG Ego

E = EQUAL Ego

S = SMALL Ego

Where do you communicate from most frequently and/or most comfortably?

You might recognize your "BIG ego" when demonstrating your authority, providing directions or instructions, reprimanding or being judgmental. Sometimes it's necessary to be highly directive (emergencies and dangerous situations), but you may have noticed that when inappropriately **telling** people what to do…*in word or action*, the other often responds from their SMALL ego state. This is obvious in interactions between parents and teenagers!

The "SMALL ego state" is noticeable when we become emotional, defensive, blame, lash out, retreat, defer to others or gather strength by gossiping.

The "EQUAL ego state" is when we are respectful, equally engaged and engaging, listening, thinking, considering and valuing other opinions. It is when we come away from an interaction and all parties feel energized, valued and validated even through disagreement.

What's interesting about this theory is that when we speak from a "BIG ego state", the person we interact with can easily slip into their "SMALL ego state". That's all it takes to create defensiveness, diminishing the effectiveness of the communication. The words might have been great, but the delivery questionable. The reverse is also true. When approaching another from the "SMALL ego state", deferring to them inappropriately, not taking personal responsibility or accountability we can nudge the other into their "BIG ego state" of telling or superiority…the very demeanor we don't like about them!

 After being immersed in Coach Training I was keen to try this concept in many areas of my life. I noticed how many times parents tangle with young children and wanted to experiment. When caring for my three-year-old granddaughter, Isabella, she was playing with several coasters in my living room. Some of those coasters were glass, some were cork…the floor was hardwood! A normal reaction to a toddler playing with something dangerous is taking it away (most likely starting a war!) or distracting the child and then taking it away or launching into a diatribe of the dangers of that item.

This time I chose to say "Isabella, some of those are dangerous to play with and some are not. Which ones do you think are dangerous?" She stopped playing, examined the coasters and pointed to all those that were glass. I then asked what we should do with the glass coasters. She brought each one to me with no fuss or resistance. Given the freedom to choose, she chose well. I didn't have to be as directive as one would think. Giving others the ability to move into their "EQUAL state" (at almost any age or stage of life) brings the rewards of thinking and accountability.

Notice that you will likely be able to identify the alter ego state of other people, in fact it's kind of a fun study! It's a great start (especially if you can do it without judgment!) but as always your challenge in the **PMS** process is to notice **your own** state in communication and to understand how you impact and affect others!

I grew up in a family where voices were seldom raised and people tended to get angry and leave rather than work through disagreements. My husband on the other hand grew up in a family where yelling was just part of the ordinary day. Our greatest challenge has been to develop our own communication style where we both feel heard without the

Possibility Mind Shift

need for raised voices. He has made a great effort to monitor the tone and volume of his voice when speaking to me about matters he feels strongly about. I have worked hard to stay present when we have a disagreement. It is a work in progress, and I am very aware of the effort it has taken.

Communication is a BIG subject!! What you say and how you listen are only part of the equation for effective communication. Tone of voice, volume of speech, body language and eye contact are also incredibly important. Becoming more self-aware of how you present yourself, and how the other person reacts can be very helpful in maintaining and growing effective communication styles. And we never have to stop learning about it…

The first three months of the two-year Career Facilitator Certificate program I was taking at Okanagan College was on Communication. I had been teaching Communication courses at the college level for over ten years, so asked if I could forgo the first three months…the answer was "no"! One of the continuous assignments was to journal each week on a component of Communication we were focusing on, and hand in our journals to the instructor. My "halo" was shining from the pages as I described how I "always did this", and "paid attention to that", demonstrating how well I was doing in in my daily communication. After about three of these assignments, the instructor jotted a note in the margin…" Anita, I wonder if there is <u>something </u>that you might learn from this program?" That was both the most humiliating and illuminating learning moment in my life! I realized then my "knowingness" was getting in the way of my learning and growing. I learned more about Communication in that three months than I had ever learned about the subject previously. I'm forever grateful for that humbling moment…I was converted into a true learner that day!

Under what circumstances are you more likely to slip out of your most appropriate communication state?

....
....
....
....
....
....
....
....
....
....
....
....
....
....
....
....
....
....
....
....
....
....
....
....
....

Possibility Mind Shift

What are you noticing about the effectiveness of your listening skills?

....

....

....

....

....

....

....

....

....

....

....

....

....

....

....

....

....

....

....

....

....

....

....

....

....

....

Week 12:

Set Boundaries and Goals... But Don't Take Yourself Too Seriously!

Who is the director of your life?

Do you control your own actions and how you choose to spend your time or do other people manage that for you?

When you think about your own life and your future intentions, consider who is really calling the shots. Are you letting your past mistakes colour your future? Are you letting the mistakes of the people in your past leave their imprint on who you are now? Consider the trajectory of your life right now, what would it look like in a year's time if you make no changes or adjustments...just slide from today into the same time a year from now? Now create a picture of what you would like for your future, including your activities, the people in your life, your daily routines, your rewards and celebrations.

How do you really want your life to play out? What decisions will give you more control of your chosen path and destination?

When we're busy living our lives, we don't always pay attention to **how** we're living it! There are many ideas and strategies that can help nudge us into awareness but we can't do all of them.

Many have grown up at a time and in families where healthy boundaries were not necessarily understood nor modeled. If we want to create them, we first must learn what they are and how to recognize them. With multiple roles and an "others first" ideology, many women in mid-life are realizing they have been living with loose or nonexistent boundaries. Even if the boundaries did exist at one time, there is a possibility they eroded through time and responsibilities. If you are feeling that everyone else's needs are being met before your own are even considered, there may be a boundary issue. If you notice that you'd rather just ignore something that normally would be important to you, or if you have a consistent, nagging feeling of discomfort in the presence of some people, it may be that your boundaries need attention.

In her book "*Boundaries: Where You End and I Begin*", author Anne Katherine defines a boundary as:

> "...a limit or edge that defines you as separate from others. A boundary is a natural container for self. It can include the skin, a comfort zone around our body, as well as emotional, physical and relationship space. The purpose of a healthy boundary is to help us set limits, to stay separate and still be in connection with others."

Boundaries have clear and definite limits, and although there may be some flexibility depending on the people and circumstances, the healthy "edges" require your awareness and clarity.

Your boundaries are directly linked to your values. When there is a values conflict there is an opportunity to define and draw the line that contains the border of the value…that's the boundary! Revisit your values if something just doesn't feel right and you will likely find a boundary violation.

When I was a younger woman, I had a great deal of difficulty in saying "No" to others. I learned when I said yes to something, I was in essence saying "No" to something else as there was only so much of me to go around. I learned to pause and think about my response, checking in with myself before I committed to something. This helped me learn what my priorities and values really were and allowed me to set boundaries in a systematic manner.

Boundaries can be felt emotionally and physically. We know when someone is physically too close to us and have a natural tendency to step away. We don't always pick up on that as easily when the proximity is emotional rather than physical…for example when others are simply too demanding. To reconnect with your most natural ability and to really know your boundaries, listen to your body and let your natural instincts be your guide.

In her book "*Untamed*", Glennon Doyle describes boundaries as: "*the edge of one of our root beliefs about ourselves and the world.*" Often beliefs are programmed by our culture, community, religion or family. Sometimes what feels like a boundary violation may no longer actually fit for us and so it is important to really dig deep at those times and consider what you actually do believe.

Having healthy boundaries and being aware of them can help you grow.

In working through the whole **PMS** process, we hope that you can learn and grow with levity.

There's a growing body of evidence showing laughter is the best medicine, yet just when we need it the most it seems our prescription runs out!

Laughter can help bring perspective to difficult situations. It can bring some sense of meaning to the absurd. Laughter can help us forgive ourselves for those moments we wish hadn't happened… like the "foot in the mouth" or worse! Often, time can bring glimpses of humour to problems and challenges, but is it possible to lighten up a bit sooner?

In his book "The Art of Possibility" author Ben Zander tells a story about an organizational leader who, when confronted with staff members who were frenzied, frustrated and out of control would simply say "Please, please! Remember Rule #6"! This magically and instantly restored calm. When asked by someone who witnessed this remarkable change the response was, "Oh, it just means don't take yourself so seriously"! Impressed by the results of this unusual rule the question was then asked "what are the other five rules?", the reply was, "there aren't any…there's just rule #6!"

Even when things just aren't funny, we may be able to apply this principle. When you can see the lighter side of a situation it allows some levity and light into your life, decreasing the negative emotional impact. We all need more of that!

Imagine being in a highly charged emotional moment with people who matter to you. You say something stupid and for days afterwards feel terrible about the mistake you made. Time passes and eventually you are able to see the humour in the situation, because there is humour in everything…sometimes you just have to search for it!! When you can truly laugh at yourself it is much easier to forgive and move forward. Now all you need is to do it sooner!

 Each year I escape winter with MJ, a long-term dear friend. We rent a place in California for two months for a golf getaway. Even with people we love to hang out with, two months is a long time, and although we get along great, every once in a while, things get a bit tense! MJ came up with a great solution…she suggested that "any time I want to call you a bitch, I'll just call you a wizard, and then no one else will know!" We get a lot of laughter out of this because we generally need to explain it to anyone who hears one of us use that term.

Laughter helps you look at things through a different lens. It changes how you see yourself and allows you to see another's perspective more easily.

With our sense of humour intact and boundaries clearly defined, Goal Setting is the next important skill. Setting SMART goals provides a measurable way to determine your success.

S = Specific. What exactly will you accomplish?
M = Measurable. How will you know when you have reached this goal?
A = Attainable. Is this a goal that you can reach with the effort, resources and time you have available?
R = Realistic. Why is this goal significant to you? Make it achievable or you'll set yourself up to fail.
T = Timely. When will you achieve this goal?

For example, one of our goals is:

We will have this **PMS** book submitted to the publisher by November 2020.

Being able to "nudge" your intentions from duty to delight may change how you create your future. There is a very subtle difference that changes our chances of success. The weight loss program motivated by the wonderful feeling of levity and increased energy will have a different outcome than the one driven by negative feelings about yourself.

It's all about tapping into a positive feeling that you have had in the past and linking that to the goal you are considering.

What other goals might you consider setting?

....

....

....

....

....

....

....

....

....

....

....

....

....

....

....

....

....

....

....

....

....

....

....

....

Identify one area in your life where you take yourself too seriously? How can you lighten up?

....

....

....

....

....

....

....

....

....

....

....

....

....

....

....

....

....

....

....

....

....

....

....

....

....

Week 13:

Increasing Awareness in the Job of Living

Are you living to work or working to live?

When we refer to work we usually connect that with a phase of our life that produces an income. So, what is your work? Is it the activity you go to every day and receive a paycheck for or is it a volunteer task you are involved in? Is it keeping your garden well-groomed or is it looking after your children or grandchildren? We are referring to work as the "job of living" regardless of your age or stage of life.

Quality of life is sadly diminished when our careers result in daily dissatisfaction over long periods of time. Sometimes work just isn't fun or fulfilling but we have to continue to work to pave the way into a career. What would it be like to really, really enjoy that daily activity called "work"? As your focus moves to the subject of the "Job of Living", it might be an interesting process to examine how well suited your communication needs and style are to your current circumstances and aspirations.

There was a time when people toiled their entire life dreaming of what they would do when they retired. They set aside their interests, disliked their work and were too tired to enjoy their time off. When they retired with their gold watch, they became unhappy, ill and too soon, passed away. Some people though, died before they died...and that was often due to their dissatisfaction in their daily job of living!

> *"The key to immortality is first to live a life worth remembering."*
> *~ Bruce Lee~*

Some people give up every part of their life for their work or career, eroding social and personal relationships, and wear this commitment to their job as a badge of honour. They may be seen by some as loyal employees, but is it causing them to become unhappy and dissatisfied instead of providing the richness in their lives that they really want?

It would be an interesting study to find out how others view this subject. This is a new time in a world that offers multiple choices and opportunities to create careers that have never before been available.

> *"As long as you are trying to be something other than what you actually are,*
> *your mind wears itself out."*
> *~ J. Krishnamurti ~*

Take another look at how you measured your "Career or Work" segment on your Indicator Wheel in Week Three. Notice how you define that segment. It is often associated with wages or salary, but a career can be life work that is rewarded in other ways. There are people who opt for parenting, volunteerism, or family caregiving as their chosen careers.

Assessment and measurement of your work or career is not always easy because it's a challenge to know what to use as comparative benchmarks. Often people only consider their careers when they are unhappy with their work, in transition, or unemployed.

When I worked at the hospital, I felt unfulfilled and found working in a large system difficult. I have never responded well when other people tell me what to do and when I have trouble respecting those individuals it was even worse. However, I had two small children at home and my husband was a self-employed farmer. My options felt limited! I opened a private practice while still employed part time at two different hospitals. I was able to gradually build up my business and after four years transitioned working fulltime in private practice. Now thirty years later, I know if I had remained in the hospital environment, I would be able to retire with a good pension. However, I really feel I would be receiving that pension in the psychiatric ward. I have had an amazing career with all sorts of opportunities that I never would have experienced had I remained in the public health system.

Career Buffet ~ Check out what is being served!

Strategies for tweaking, designing or re-designing careers are like a cruise ship buffet…there are endless possibilities. A question asked by a **PMS** participant was "what if, in this process I find out that I really hate my job… what do I do then?" The answer is first of all, don't ignore that important realization. Take it seriously, or you may end up being the "boiled frog" featured in Week One! Know discomfort and awareness are important first stages in change. Not many people are in a position to just quit, so if you find yourself squirming, you're in good company. There are endless resources including books, career counselors and coaches to help you get create a specific plan.

> **"Learn to be what you are and learn to resign**
> **with a good grace all that you are not."**
> ~ *Henri Frederic Amiel*~

Instead of quickly leaping into another job that may result in the pattern of contributing to a negative career history, choose a more thoughtful and purposeful process. One that will have a greater potential for success and long-term satisfaction. We can learn from others as we hear their stories…

A forty-something self-employed flooring specialist found himself feeling unfulfilled and depressed with his chosen career even though he loved the artistry and physical work. After some career exploration and self-reflective exercises, he found that what was missing was working with people. He then adjusted his business to include larger contracts so he could work with others and found the work satisfaction he had been looking for.

Good thing he didn't quit! To just take a blind leap out of something can have us leaping into something worse!

Possibility Mind Shift

> *"If you don't know where you are going,*
> *you might wind up someplace else."*
> *~ Yogi Berra~*

Do you feel respected and valued at work?

How do you show the people in your orbit that you respect them?

Many people working in organizations are tired of political intrigue and maneuverings that detract from the satisfaction of what their jobs could really offer them. There are people who work in the school systems and love the children they work with but hate the pettiness. There are those who work in hospitals and love dealing with the patients, but may have problems with administration. They are waiting for someone else to fix it which inadvertently diminishes their personal power.

What if all the individuals working in these organizations started treating each other with great respect and kindness? Would these issues change?

> *Consider the story of the declining monastery where the members were getting older and older, with no new members joining. One old monk went to visit his friend the rabbi and they consoled each other with conversations of how the young people were no longer interested in the monastic life. On leaving his friend, the monk asked the rabbi for advice and the rabbi replied that all he knew was that the savior lived at the monastery. When the old monk returned to the monastery, he told the other monks what the rabbi had said. Everyone wondered: "Who could be the savior? Was it old Brother John, who looked after the garden? Was it the old Prior who was so wise? Or could it be one of them?" They started treating themselves and each other with great respect as they never knew who the savior could be. Soon an air of great serenity and kindness lay around the monastery and people started to come and visit. Young people would bring picnics up to the grounds and spend time talking to the old monks. Soon some young men decided to join this community and not too many years after that initial visit the monastery was a thriving community once again.*

Each one of us has the power to change the groups and organizations we are involved in through our own behaviour and attitudes.

Even if you do not feel particularly respectful, if you act in that manner, eventually that feeling will come to you.

Consider how you could make your workplace more like the one you would really love to work in. What respectful and caring gestures can you make to one of your colleagues today?

Do you wake up on Monday morning looking forward to going to work, or do you remember what day it is and lose your enthusiasm?

Increased demands in the workplace will make it more likely you will experience some level of "burn-out". Think about the word "burn-out". It suggests that like an engine or a light bulb our energy is depleted! We need to pay attention and manage ourselves better before that energy really is completely exhausted.

Here's a scenario you might relate to.

> *For the most part you usually like your work. The people are great but you are finding yourself increasingly frustrated by the politics and hidden agendas. It seems you are walking through a workplace minefield. There is a sense of dread at the thought of Monday mornings. One day you realize you feel physically ill at work. You might notice that you are looking for escapes to "hideaway" and deal with your frequent headaches, heartburn or sick stomach. You might notice this doesn't happen at home, and you come to the realization your work is actually making you sick.*

Sound familiar? You may have the option of changing jobs, however ultimately there is going to be stress wherever you work, so why not learn to manage it better?

- o Awareness. Get to know what the underlying cause of the stress is. Is it really a workload issue or perhaps it's a communication breakdown or a values conflict?
- o Assess what is on your plate. Determine what you can let go of and what you might need to delegate or get help with?
- o Access support. Some people find it difficult to ask for help but creating collaborative relationships can develop into a powerful support network for yourself and others.
- o Re-charge and regenerate. Find some time for yourself every day to ensure proper nutrition, rest, exercise and some true enjoyment.

What do you do if you identify a values conflict?

Sometimes there are applications of values that seemingly contradict one's career choices. For instance, a financial advisor who does not place a high value on money. She may find a way to specifically align her practice to better serve her clients' personal values by helping them invest in funds representing causes close to their hearts.

We have discussed ideas such as personality inventories and other factors that may impact choices in your job of living. Consider how you reacted in the previous modules and how those factors may influence you in your day to day activities.

Consider your educational and skill development needs at any age or stage. What might you want to invest in? Education is now more accessible through new and creative distributed learning processes. No longer do we need to stop working to engage in exceptional educational programs at all levels. Learn while you earn and apply this knowledge to your current work and life circumstances. A woman who feared that she was too old to go back to school wrote to a counsellor saying it's a four-year course and she'd be 45 by the time she got her degree. The counsellor responded, "and how old will you be if you don't get your degree?"

You are unique and valuable. Discover all that you have to give and know what brings you the greatest satisfaction…that probably means you're really good at it! Don't be humble – give your gifts to the world now!

During a recent workshop these concepts were discussed and a participant was absolutely shocked and bewildered that anyone would even think about work as being satisfying. This was a woman in her late 50's who said she had always just worked to pay the bills. It had never occurred to her that she might consider enjoying or valuing her work, aside from having a few laughs with co-workers once in a while. She had always focused on the mechanics of her job, and when she got home, she was usually exhausted. Some people in that same workshop, doing the same work, loved their job feeling energized and rewarded through the service they provided. Yet there are many who are being drained and used up by their work, diminishing the quality of their lives.

What one thing could you start doing right now that would make a difference to how you feel in your job of living?

....

....

....

....

....

....

....

....

....

....

....

....

....

....

....

....

....

....

....

....

....

....

....

If you could create or recreate your meaningful activities what would they look like?

....

....

....

....

....

....

....

....

....

....

....

....

....

....

....

....

....

....

....

....

....

....

....

....

Week 14:

Creating Community

In years past people lived in neighborhoods where they all knew each other. They would have people over for coffee, share meals and care for each other's children. They knew everyone who lived close by and developed significant relationships, flaws and all! With the busy lives we live now and the number of times people move, this "community" scenario is less familiar. How many of your neighbors do you know? How do you now define community? Is it where you live or what you share in common?

Likely you've noticed community is not just about where you live. A community can be a group of like-minded people with a similar interest or goal. It can be the hiking club, a spiritual or religious organization or a professional or alumni group. It can be people with children of the same age or those with similar interests.

There are many other types of communities. Some housing developments intentionally build a structure to create "community". Potential tenants are interviewed to ensure they understand the shared expectations for living there. There are events organized for the whole community and a structure that both supports involvement and respects privacy. This type of living arrangement is not for everyone but many people truly thrive in it and enjoy the fact that they know and interact regularly with others in their community.

Community is built on the sharing of common values and a commitment of time, interest and energy. Whatever the community, the individuals in it have an unspoken agreement with an informal pact to care for one another. Whether it is an intention to build a good child care system, provide a time to relax with like-minded people or work hard to build a professional identity, the ideal community provides the opportunity to be an integral part of a healthier and respectful world.

What are the communities in your life? How has their role changed over the years as you've moved, changed jobs and developed new relationships?

There are numerous get-a-ways, summer camps, music, art and dance workshops and retreats that bring people together where they bond in ways deeper and stronger than many long-term relationships. These special events share common attributes that contribute to a strong sense of community. Generally, there are little or no techno-interferences, a specific shared interest and very few artificial barriers like corporate positions and three-piece suits! They are typically facilitated to break barriers and create common and long-lasting bonds.

In the early 1990's I discovered the Puget Sound Guitar Workshop, (PSGW). This is a camp for adults held for three weeks every summer in the woods of the Puget Sound. I went alone the first time and was surrounded by talented musicians and people with the same interest as I had in writing songs, singing and playing music. I cried all the way home as I had discovered kindred souls I had never thought I would meet and wondered if that experience would ever be repeated. Over the years as I have continued to attend, I have made my everyday life more like the life at camp. Many of my good friends are people I met at PSGW and I play a lot more music now than I ever did.

PSGW is a very important community to me! I now make an effort to keep in touch with my friends from camp, getting together several times a year to visit and play music. I have a band in my own community and organize a "jam" session once a month at my house. Now I don't have to wait for that one week in the summer to have a musical community around me.

Our world is changing. Cyber-communities are now part of our global culture…people connecting on-line through a broad reach that spans our world. Some of these community relationships are satisfying in many ways but leave an empty hole of real human to human contact.

We live in a society where independence is encouraged and respected which brings some to the conclusion that the relationship of community is not necessary. However, we clearly see the negative impact of loneliness when we experienced the Covid19 isolation.

In his book "*Social Intelligence*" Daniel Goleman reports that "*Neuroscience has discovered that our brain's very design makes it sociable, inexorably drawn into an intimate brain-to-brain link up whenever we engage with another person. That neural bridge lets us affect the brain – and so the body – of everyone we interact with, just as they do us.*"

In other words, we have a physiological **need** for community and belonging! It can be small or large, close or far… and *it can be created and/or enhanced.*

Are you satisfied with the communities you are involved with?

Your level of satisfaction with your community involvement needs to be evaluated in a way that makes sense to you. One way to evaluate the importance of the communities you belong to is to do a values check. How do the values exhibited by the community compare to the ones you have recognized as important to you? Are you drained or energized by them? What can you do to decrease the negatives and increase the positive effects?

It is important to identify the communities that are part of your life and determine how they impact you. If you realize that you are only involved out of a sense of duty or obligation then it may be time to go back and have another look at your Wheel of Life!

To examine and reflect on community, four focus areas are offered here for your consideration. Different strategies are provided for each option to help in designing your process to attain the desired outcomes. You might choose to give attention to more than one of these areas or give your full attention to one. Ideally, the intention is to create the community that has the greatest impact on you and your personal satisfaction.

1. ***If you want to decrease involvement in your current community or communities:***
People can outgrow the community they have been a part of and, like the message from the "boiled frog" suggests, they may not realize how they are slowly being used up by the demands of that group while there is diminishing reciprocity. Take a look in the rear-view mirror!

- Be honest…with yourself and then with the community. Be clear about why you have to change or move on and then respectfully provide the rationale if you feel it's necessary.
- Share with those close to you what you have learned, how they have helped shape who you are and what you now offer the world.
- Plan your graceful exit with a specific timeline.
- Or just delete those emails!

2. ***If you want to increase satisfaction in your current community or communities:***
Often people become complacent in their community over time, taking for granted the importance of the purpose and their role in it.
- Look with new eyes and note the benefits and positive aspects.
- Identify your commitment to the purpose and your role in it.
- Clarify and capture what satisfaction and reward you get from involvement.
- Create a plan to make a more meaningful contribution and offer renewed energy.

3. ***If you want to move into an existing community:***
- Be clear about why you are attracted to or feel connected to this group.
- Know how the people, the activities and the community are meaningful to you.
- Have clarity about what you can contribute and what satisfaction you will get from this community.

4. ***Or, create a new community that will serve you and that you can contribute to:***
There may be a need for a community that does not yet exist for your specific needs. We have seen people who have suffered the loss of a loved one create a new community through the passion of their grief. Some of these quite literally changed the world!

"Never doubt that a small, group of thoughtful, committed citizens can change the world. Indeed, it is the only thing that ever has."
~ Margaret Mead~

What community is important to you to be a part of?

....

....

....

....

....

....

....

....

....

....

....

....

....

....

....

....

....

....

....

....

....

....

....

....

....

....

Imagine what your community might look like a year from now. What do you need to do to make that a reality?

....

....

....

....

....

....

....

....

....

....

....

....

....

....

....

....

....

....

....

....

....

....

....

....

Possibility Mind Shift

Week 15:

What about your Environment?

The intention of this module is to create a plan to help you become aware of how the different environments you live and work in support and nurture you, and how you can support and nurture them.

How has your environment created you and how are you creating it? We're talking about your environment in the smallest and the largest sense of the word. It is your room or home, your city and country, and it is this beautiful planet we all share. Think deeply about how your surroundings affect you and your impact on them. Consider how the environment you are creating represents who you are.

Starting with your home, become a detective looking for clues for a profile or the traits and characteristics of the person who lives there. Look with new eyes at your surroundings. Are the inhabitants calm and laid back or active and energetic? Consider the lighting, is it bright or muted, are there magazines and books, blankets and pillows, knick-knacks and candles? Is it friendly or private, clutter or clear, warm or cool?

Imagine unexpected visitors stopping by. Does your environment support the person you are? Is it an accurate representation of you? Look around with fresh eyes and see what they would see. The point of this discussion is not about housekeeping, but about what you find most comfortable and nurturing.

On the continuum of "clinically clean to cluttered" you'll find your comfort and your nurturing spot. You may have a "nesting" environment, which might include books, blankets, a candle and a cozy corner to read. Or it could be a cluttered room with many of those same items and many more! Your environment will likely be having an impact on the quality of your life. Only you will know what's best for you. What do you need to move closer to the environment that will support you in the very best way?

If you're a "neat freak" with a large home, you're likely spending a great deal of time and energy maintaining it. If cleaning is one of your stress management strategies and you feel satisfied or energized when you've vacuumed, scrubbed and dusted, then it may be working well for you. If you're that same tidy person in a home you just don't have the time to maintain it could be wearing you out. And what about that car? Filled with fast food wrappers and fingerprints that put the brakes on your energy…*how is that serving you!?*

> *"My home is not a place,*
> *it is people."*
> ~ Lois McMaster Bujold ~

Consider the other environments that are consistent parts of your life? Is your work environment one that supports you and the others you share it with? Is it providing more than just a productive place to work?

Our environment extends outward, and most of it is shared. We can't change what others are doing, but we can lead by example and do our part to be responsible and accountable to our shared home…*Planet Earth*.

With a more universal focus on leaving a smaller carbon footprint and the concern about global warming, "environment" takes on a much bigger meaning. It means planning on how you can make a difference to decrease the negative impact. We need to be concerned about how we can make a positive difference in the world we are leaving for our children and grandchildren.

Imagine a child hunting through your home for the things that will have a negative impact on the world. Look through that child's eyes and see if you can find at least one more change you can make to contribute to a healthier environment. What can you do to feel like you're contributing or supporting the environmental concerns of the world? Only *you* know the answers to these questions. What is your assessment?

> ***"There are no passengers on Spaceship Earth.***
> ***We are all crew."***
> *~Marshall McLuhan ~*

Using an appreciative approach, focus on the positive attributes of your favourite places and consider creating more. What is it about those places you love? Examine the details; is it the light, the space, the activity, the people or the lack of clutter!? The differences might be the homey touches or the photos of the people you love. Notice the factors that make you feel good in those places.

Think about the sensory approach and capture in writing the sights, sounds, smells and feelings you want more of.

> ***"I long, as does every human being,***
> ***to be at home wherever I find myself."***
> *~ Maya Angelou~*

In 1986 my husband and I bought a neglected ten-acre farm with a very old, rundown farm house just north of Oliver. Over the years he has made it into a beautiful retreat with a lovely timber frame home and a handmade labyrinth for walking meditation. It is an oasis for our family. However, it is also a lot of work! We decided in 2020 to retire, sell our property and travel the world.

In 1988 we purchased a very small and primitive cabin at Mount Baldy and over the years have spent a lot of time up there. It too has been renovated and made more comfortable but it was still a cabin with no cupboards and little privacy. In 2019 we decided to renovate our cabin to become our primary residence. This has allowed us to keep much of our family history as although the cabin is now renovated into a "chalet" it holds many memories. My husband used all the wood from the old cabin, recycling it into the new structure and it has many hand-worked features much like our home.

Although it will be difficult to leave our beautiful property in the valley, moving to our long-term recreational property will make that move easier. I have been acutely aware of this over the last year as we started the renovation and thought about what we would want in our new "forever home".

I have two homes…one with my boyfriend and my own place that my son and his daughter are currently occupying. My home is relatively new with a décor that is open, bright and uncluttered. The theme represents freedom, future possibility, family, socialization and music.

My boyfriend is a collector of sports and music memorabilia, antique furniture and one of a kind dishes and cutlery…each one with a story of where it came from. I love his place for the character and although I have helped to "decorate" to a certain extent, it clearly has his touch reflecting an appreciation of history. It is an old home and has a huge yard with a private beach. I love the relaxed lifestyle of this lake home and my time with him is precious. However, I also love my own place.

I recognize that I am very high on the "flexibility" continuum, so can make myself happy and comfortable wherever I am, even for long periods of time. But the crunch comes when we talk about selling and moving in together permanently. I am in the midst of decluttering and considering a move to a shared home. The cleaning and purging is cathartic, but that activity is making me realize our two very different environment styles are creating some anxiety.

I can appreciate and even love his environment…but it is definitely not representative of who I am. So, I continue to move through the process of learning more about what I need in my environment and what I need to do to look after myself in this relationship. The work never stops!

What environment needs your attention?

....
....
....
....
....
....
....
....
....
....
....
....
....
....
....
....
....
....
....
....
....
....
....
....
....

What one thing could you do right now to make one of the environments you lived in more satisfying?

....

....

....

....

....

....

....

....

....

....

....

....

....

....

....

....

....

....

....

....

....

....

....

....

Week 16:

Evaluating your Health

In order to change we must be sick and tired
of being sick and tired.
~ Author Unknown ~

Imagine that your body is like your car. You are driving along when you suddenly notice the yellow "check engine" light is on. Yikes!! You quickly pull over and call your mechanic who suggests you come in for a checkup. He assures you it is a minor problem and not to pay any attention to it. You continue on your trip overlooking the light, even when someone asks you about it. You explain it away as nothing to worry about. How does this make you feel? What happens if an additional problem arises that does require some attention? How will you know?

The analogy of the yellow light can be used to describe early warning signals of stress in our bodies. Imagine you are feeling very tired and headachy. You notice you tend to feel this way when you are under pressure at work or faced with a deadline. Once you realize what it is and identify it as a minor problem, you choose to ignore it. Explained away, you might even stop noticing it altogether. You have just stopped paying attention to your "yellow check engine light"!! What happens when there is another problem or the stress increases to the point where you are causing serious physical damage to your precious vehicle? Are you overlooking something that may be important?

Pay attention to your early warning signals and how you manage stress. Some people hold stress in the neck and shoulder areas which may cause pain and headaches. Others clench their jaws causing dental damage and jaw pain or carry it in their stomach and digestive systems. If you take your warning lights seriously you can then choose to make some appropriate changes.

Looking back on your Indicator Wheel from Week Three, what did your segment on health look like? Does it look a bit different now that you are more aware? Circumstances will affect your response to the question of what health means to you. For instance, when a person close to us is diagnosed with a new health condition, we pay attention differently. When we were initially faced with Covid 19, we took stock of and paid attention to our health in a new way.

We are fortunate to be living in a time when we have access to more information and options, but it is important to become aware of ourselves and our state of health so we can make the most appropriate choices.

Over the years there have been several definitions of "health". The medical model has been dominant in North America and focuses on the idea that the body is like a machine to be fixed when broken. It emphasizes treating specific physical disease but does not accommodate mental or social problems well. Treating and medicating the health *problems*, often de-emphasizes prevention. This has led to measuring health by an absence of disease and focuses on the smooth functioning of all physical body systems.

Another model that defines health is the <u>holistic model</u> presented by the World Health Organization in 1948 as *"a state of complete physical, mental and social well-being, and not merely the absence of disease or infirmity."* This is not exactly a current definition but it is a true and accurate statement. This *model is* more vague and harder to measure as it becomes more subjective at the individual level. However, it extends beyond just physical problems occurring and recognizes both mental and social factors are important components of the overall state of one's health.

A third definition is the <u>wellness model</u>. In 1984 the World Health Organization proposed moving away from health as a static state and proposed it is a dynamic interaction between the person, the environment and society. This introduced the concepts of resiliency and recovery, allowing those who have "health issues" such as a spinal cord injury to still be regarded as being healthy. Who could consider a force like Rick Hansen not to be full of health? Yet when considered within the medical model, a person with a spinal cord lesion would not be thought of in that way.

Should one focus so exclusively on health that the pleasure in life is impacted? We are inundated with health information through the media providing advice on what is good for us and what isn't. Many people become unhappy with how much they weigh and how they look by comparison to the "media beauty model". Listen to yourself in a respectful and non-judgmental way and you will know what you need to be healthy. Don't wait for a health crisis before taking action on a health issue. You can create your own template for what you **know** is healthy **for you, and you can do it NOW!**

> *If I'd known I was going to live so long,*
> *I'd have taken better care of myself.*
> *~ Leon Eldred ~*

Health affects every aspect of your life whether you're aware of it or not. Decide which model of health you want to embrace and then determine what you want and need to do in order to meet your health goals?

There are an abundance of articles, apps and methods designed to provide advice on maintaining your health. This process should take you deeper than that. We are inviting you to take a serious and meaningful look at your health.

This medical model list of health questions is modified with a coach approach. Reflect on them …some of them are easy and some might require more time and thought.

- ❑ Do you smoke? How important is that to you?
- ❑ How do you exercise? How often?
- ❑ How much sleep do you get per night?
- ❑ How often do you get a complete physical checkup?
- ❑ How often do you eat fast food?
- ❑ How much fruit do you eat per day?
- ❑ How many vegetables do you eat daily?
- ❑ What is your blood pressure? What do you need to know about it?
- ❑ What are your cholesterol rates? What do you need to learn about cholesterol?
- ❑ What is your ideal weight? What is the gap?
- ❑ What is your intake of alcohol? What is the right balance for you?
- ❑ How often do you do a breast self-examination? Mammogram?

Here are some questions focusing on the holistic or wellness model.
Consider using a scale of 1 – 10 to evaluate these areas:

- ❑ How happy are you with your job?
- ❑ How is the health of your primary relationship?
- ❑ What is your level of satisfaction in your relationship with yourself?
- ❑ What is your level of ability to relax?
- ❑ What is your ability in terms of managing your time well?
- ❑ What is your level of joy or satisfaction?
- ❑ How often do you have a belly laugh?

What other questions might you ask yourself that are important to your state of health?

We all know what we "should" be doing to live a healthy life, but how many of us really do what needs to be done? What one or two things are most important for **you** to address?

Eat right, exercise regularly, die anyway.
~Author Unknown~

PMS says…

Eat right, exercise regularly, laugh often
and enjoy a good quality of life…then die!

For some it is overwhelming to know where to start. But, like every change we make, it starts with one small step. How are you going to determine what area of your health you want to focus on and what that one small step might be?

Some know immediately what area(s) need attention. The obvious ones might be to quit smoking, reduce calorie intake, get more exercise or get more sleep. When considering some deeper or more complex issues you may need more time to reflect or observe yourself in action. Make it a priority to hold on to this focus if you have not figured it out yet…your health won't wait for you! So, be good to yourself and give your health the attention it deserves.

When you **know** what you want to work on it is important to make your plan manageable, enjoyable, satisfying and rewarding. Your plan has to be attainable and successful from the start and you are the only one who knows what your personal plan needs to be!

"My own prescription for health is less paperwork and
more running barefoot through the grass."
~ Leslie Grimutter ~

Whatever you decide on it might be helpful to use the **S.M.A.R.T.** goal setting process (from Week 12!). Take some time to write your goals in your journal and commit to them.

What are your warning lights?

What will you choose to do when the lights come on?

Don't lose your head,

Just make your goals SMART ones!

What does Health mean to you?

....

....

....

....

....

....

....

....

....

....

....

....

....

....

....

....

....

....

....

....

....

....

....

....

Possibility Mind Shift

What is one SMART goal you can focus on this week to improve your health?

Week 17:

Let's have some FUN!!

*"We don't stop playing
because we grow old,
We grow old because
we stop playing."*
~ Satchel Paige ~

What did your balance wheel indicate when you looked at the segment measuring leisure or fun activities? It may be something that needs your attention. There might have been some subtle messages you absorbed over the years. You may have heard people in positions of authority tell you to "grow up", "don't act silly", and "act your age" *…whatever that means*! With these messages in our heads, it may be hard work for some of us to play! So, the question is, does play drain your energy, or does it energize and refresh you?

First of all, it's important to define what those fun and leisure activities are. For some of us working is fun but that can be a double-edged sword. When we love what we do we can get ever so slowly burnt out by choosing not to get away from it at all. That old adage, "a change is as good as a rest" may be the wisdom we need to take a break from what we love. If you are in the midst of a project you feel passionate about and you like the people you are working with, it can be a lot of fun to bring it to completion. For some learning is fun, and you spend every spare minute reading a book on the latest theory or pursuing a graduate degree for pleasure! Or maybe you just aren't having any fun at all…*Ouch!*

It's surprising how easily we can become caught up in the "seriousness" of our lives. Our careers, parental roles and financial responsibilities, among other things, can lead us far away from the pleasures of a "balanced" life. Week Three, brought us to a better understanding of balance, but what about fun?

Anita had an experience that shifted her thinking and the message was delivered in a way as big and loud as the roar of a jet engine…

I was exhausted after a long work-week away from home and just wanted to be alone on the plane. The woman coming down the aisle was 74 years old and legally blind, and the flight attendant ushered her directly to the seat next to me. It was obvious she would be a chatty one, and she sure was!

She recalled her first husband was a terrible bore, but she still managed to teach him to dance. Her second husband didn't know how to dance, but she made that a condition when they were dating and it became their passion. She lost her sight several years before, but that didn't stop her from living and loving life. She couldn't see, but her husband described the scenery when they traveled, and when they danced, she could just feel and hear with no need to see.

What **joy** *she described! It was easy to become engaged in the life-story of this incredible woman. Her enthusiasm and zest for life was spilling over and I was breathing it in and becoming energized. There was a moment's pause as she reflected and gazed with sightless eyes through the small aircraft window and with a smile on her youthful 74-year-old face she asked "…and what do you do for fun?" I gasped at the question. A response would have been easy and instant had the question been "what do you do for a living?" But what about fun?!! How is it that we have placed such importance on what we do to earn money but diminished that which brings joy?*

That dancing blind lady delivered a gift that day….one that you can share if you choose to! What do **you** do for fun?

If we define a fun or leisure activity as something that provides energy and brings you joy or a deep sense of renewal it may help to narrow down which activities really are fun. If you love cooking and are hosting a family dinner (which is supposed to be a leisure activity), but it turns out that it's actually an exercise in patience and strained relationships, it doesn't count!

When the fun faces become warrior masks…it's not fun!

Another way to think about fun is to consider how it demonstrates the values you identified as important in Week Two. How are these values revealed in the activities you identified as "fun"? Consider your activities this past week (or during an average week). It might be helpful to identify how much of your day is made up of interests you find recharging and energizing. As you become more consciously aware of your activities, see if you can discover how many of these "fun" interests are actually draining and leave you dreading them. Over time you may notice that some activities that you used to find energizing or fun no longer are…we change!

Here's a tool to help evaluate those activities. See what you can learn about yourself and fun!

Activity	Energy ▲	Energy ▼	Time	Value/s Involved	Fun or Work
e.g. Reading	✓		2 hrs./wk.	Learning	Fun

What do you notice when you look at the list of your activities?

> ➢ How many of them are energy draining?
> ➢ How many of them do you look forward to and enjoy?
> ➢ How many leave you relieved when they are completed?
> ➢ What do you notice has changed over time?

What does your reaction to these questions tell you about the different activities and how they add to your "fun quotient"?

In our view you can never have too much fun! When was the last time you heard someone say, "I'm sick and tired of having so much fun?!" So, the next challenge is figuring out how you can get more of it in your life.

Remember in Week 13 we defined work as much more than "paid work". Consider your beliefs about work and play. Work is such a valued activity in our lives that some people are unable to define themselves without using their work as a descriptor. This creates major problems with life stage, age and circumstances. Some feel seriously diminished without their paid work! Why not think about building more fun into your life now and make it a joyful habit.

People adopt various strategies to incorporate more fun into their lives. Week 7 provided information about the MBTI. You might find some interesting observations about your preferences that will guide this "fun finding" process.

For example, Hilary's "J" preference provides a strategy that involves directly scheduling fun into her calendar. If she makes an effort to "book" a lunch, massage, or bike ride then she knows it will happen. If she waits to be spontaneous then that time is likely going to be filled by something else and it will not happen for her. Hilary has learned that one way to ensure she has some fun is to book it <u>before</u> she books work.

*Anita's challenge with a **"P"** preference is a bit different, but interestingly, has a similar outcome. Because she tends to naturally take a spontaneous and playful approach to almost everything, she can easily forget to intentionally leave work and responsibility out of some of her activities. It is natural for her to bring a sense of levity to almost everything she does, but she needs to become more conscious that "work fun" and "leisure fun" have a different impact on her life. So, the outcome is the same…she needs to consciously define her activities and sort out which ones aren't connected to responsibility and work, then schedule time for those fun activities.*

Another factor you might consider is the intention of the activity. As we relayed in a previous week, every year Hilary travels to the Puget Sound to a music camp where she meets kindred folks with shared interests and intentions – music, learning and fun. In a quest to understand why everyone experiences this "gift" of fun and leisure at that event she did a survey and asked what they thought the magic ingredients are. Those ingredients include trust, respect, openness, acceptance, support **and** an absence of responsibility! Add an environment devoid of outside negative influences (including electronic devices) …and they find the magic of fun, joy and laughter: *the refreshing, revitalizing energy of life!*

How can you build more fun into your life?

Chances are you have lots of ideas for the fun things you would like to add. We happen to live in an area abundant with endless activities and many of us only partake in them when we host others from out of town. That's when we visit a new winery, explore local trails, or paddle down the river channel.

A visitor from New York City came to the Okanagan Valley for the first time. The wineries were a great hit and lunch at the Lost Moose Lodge overlooking Penticton was a rare treat. The route to Oliver on Eastside Road provided a relaxing and wondrous tour along the lake, offering a captivating view of the natural beauty of the area. She was in awe of the magnificence of the landscape and even more impressed with all the available activities. This from someone who lives in what we refer to as the most exciting city in the world!! Sometimes we forget to savour this spectacular place we call home and take the beauty for granted.

What hidden little gem would you like to explore in your own environment?

Who are the people you want to spend time having fun with? Call them and arrange to share some time and new adventures!!

Make a list of all the things you want to do and start planning to be a tourist in your own back yard. Book the activities into your calendar and do what you need to do to make it happen. Treat your home like a cabin far away, turn off the phone and make sure you don't get side tracked by responsibilities and household chores for a while.

De-stress and play!

The Covid19 quarantine required that we stay home and stay safe. It is a real challenge at times to find ways to have fun without going out to a movie, for dinner or to visit friends. We had to make our own fun either alone or with the people we were quarantined with to follow the social distancing guidelines. This added another whole layer of challenge onto something that can be a trial at the best of times. Surprisingly we found activities we never would have considered before this forced isolation. Remember the gorilla story! It's all about what you focus on.

If you have to work too hard at having fun,
you're not really having fun…so try harder!!!

List five things you can do for fun. What's getting in the way of your doing one of them?

....

....

....

....

....

....

....

....

....

....

....

....

....

....

....

....

....

....

....

....

....

....

....

....

....

How can you flex or modify your schedule to make sure you have some more fun activities included?

....
....
....
....
....
....
....
....
....
....
....
....
....
....
....
....
....
....
....
....
....
....
....
....

Week 18:

Spirituality

What does Spirituality mean to you? Definitions of spirituality can vary from very religious to a more relaxed definition of wholeness, personal growth and well-being. Is it possible for a person to be a spiritual atheist? What are the elements of spirituality for you?

Gaining an awareness of and understanding our spiritual beliefs can be an intriguing experience. We are a product of our history and growing fully into our belief systems requires that we know what is our own.

> *Spirituality is a brave search for the truth about existence,*
> *fearlessly peering into the mysterious nature of life.*
> *~ Elizabeth Lesser ~*

In a moment of crisis what or who do you reach for? Some people find themselves praying when it is not something they would naturally have done in less stressful times. Some bargain with a "Higher Power" with statements like "If you just let me get through this then I will...." *(Add your own penalty item!)*

Being conscious of what you do in a time of crisis may create awareness of your true spiritual beliefs. Atheists might catch themselves fervently praying while members of the faithful might scorn their God when experiencing an unexplainable human crisis or injustice.

Spirituality is a very personal part of our lives. Unless we make a conscious effort to become aware of our beliefs, they may not be well defined and articulated.

 As a young teenager Hilary "shopped" religions. She was not brought up in an organized religion and was curious about many faiths. She went to services with whoever she was friends with at the time and experienced a variety of belief systems. She went to several places of worship, learning something from each one. What she found out early was that when her values were not supported in the religious teachings it helped her clarify her own beliefs.

She found her wholeness became greater with this increasing awareness. She also was able to recognize some of the values conflicts and distortions presented to her in her earlier experiences.

More recently, a book had been recommended to Hilary. She found it in a bookstore, skimmed through it and was immediately closed to the ideas because of the language used. It was so reminiscent of the negative religious experiences of her youth.

As hard as she tried, she just couldn't get into this book. She put off buying it but many people she knew and respected were talking about it and the profound impact it had on them. She eventually purchased the book because she felt she "should". But, once again, every time she attempted to read it, she was pushed away by the language and the way it was written. She finally gave it away and accepted it was simply not a book she could read at this time. The book may have provided many profound lessons but they are ones she cannot hear in the language they are written in.

There are several lessons in this story. First, spiritual lessons come from a variety of places, but because they may work for some doesn't necessarily mean they are appropriate for us all. Secondly there may be lessons to be learned if we can overcome the filters and barriers of our past. We might also need to recognize our needs, understand what we should leave behind, and determine what builds strength and wholeness in our lives.

> ***"Happiness cannot be traveled to, owned, earned, worn or consumed. Happiness is the spiritual experience of living every minute with love, grace and gratitude."***
> *~ Denis Waitley ~*

You may have been asked about your beliefs and had to explain them to others. It's a good experience that can help define beliefs more clearly. If you attend a place of worship it may be easier for you to define what you believe. Yet each person there may have a very different personal relationship with their spirituality and just assume everyone feels the same. Each of us sees this through our own lens, and through our own unique experiences and filters.

Be aware of how you live your religion or spirituality. Know what it means to you. Consider how it shows up and how you can use it to strengthen all of the areas of your life.

We are living in a diverse environment where we can respectfully share differing belief systems. We can explore with open minds and hearts the beliefs and philosophies of others as well as our own.

I was raised by parents who were against organized religion because of their own negative history at the hands of abusive religious zealots.

We had strong morals and my wise and loving parents ensured that we lived by the belief that we "do unto others as you would have others do unto you". They offered their four children, books on various religions, which we read and took an interest in; we had a healthy curiosity but were essentially agnostic... "I'll believe it when we see the proof"!

Even though we lived by high moral standards and principles, we were judged by others for not going to church, and not being "religious". Many have said there are no atheists or agnostics on their death beds...and I can honestly say that my parents lived full, happy lives, contributed to their communities and the world, and died peacefully with no eternal expectations!

Of my three siblings, I was the one most interested in the mysteries of belief systems and developed a sense of spirituality early in my life, even though I was always seeking to find scientific explanations. I continue to believe there is something "<u>more</u>" that we don't yet know or understand. Mostly I love *living in "possibility", so I am free to explore various approaches to spirituality and belief systems. However, within this process, I still retain the need to rationalize my understanding that we just don't yet know what we don't know!*

That interest has served me well. When my mother was having chemo treatments, my sister and I took a Healing Touch course to help her through her pain; it was remarkably successful! Our "scientist" father even appreciated it when he saw the benefits and was able to apply a scientific explanation of the fact that everything is energy! And I continue to question and grow into the exciting mysteries of the unknown.

We are, after all, a part of a larger integrated living system in this amazing world. Together we breath the same air, share the waters, cry tears of joy and sadness, experience the sun and the stars…we are spiritually connected.

So, what do you believe about that connectedness…how are we all sharing this world? How can we share it with a more generous and inclusive spirit?

How do you define your spirituality?

....

....

....

....

....

....

....

....

....

....

....

....

....

....

....

....

....

....

....

....

....

....

....

....

....

How do you "live" your beliefs?

Week 19:

Reflection

"The future is not somewhere we are going, but one we are creating. The paths to it are not found but made, and the activity of making them changes both the maker and the destination."
~ John Schaar ~

You are creating your life one day, one week at a time and although this **PMS** process is nearing its end, your journey is fresh and new every week for the rest of your life!

Of the subjects you've learned about or grown from the most, identify what specifically were the big shifts for you. Those big shifts may contain steppingstones to greater awareness and even bigger applications to come. Scour the subjects in previous modules and see if there are some wonderful gems still hiding there!

Consider who you were three months ago and who you have become today…notice what some of the most important changes are. Remember your life is a journey and not a destination…you'll never arrive at a perfect balance, but when you choose to, you can find great joy in making the adjustments.

You are both the masterpiece and the artist…living in a changing world. It seems even with all the work you do on yourself and on your life, you still have bumps and problems to work through. That's the good news…*you will always be in the process of creating the masterpiece of yourself!!* It is a privileged journey to travel through the years growing into the best you can be.

One of our goals has been to live the best lives possible, and as we do, we develop a template our children can follow. A new pattern so they can wisely live the best lives they can in their own time and circumstances. Allowing them to live into their own possibility is a part of our own growth!! Growth is a process and sends a strong message to the people we love the most. It's okay to make mistakes; the difficult times provide our greatest learning opportunities. But it's in those times we may be someone we don't particularly like. That's okay too…as long as we notice, and then find a way to manage the person we don't want to be.

"Remember who you are
by experiencing who you are not."

I came unglued! Unfortunately, I was emotionally charged by things other people had said to me. I had been recovering from the long illness and death of my husband after 42 years of marriage. In the following few years, I was trying to create an independent life full of things I enjoy doing. The message that came to me was that I should be more available for my grown children and I should be more accessible to take care of my grandchildren. What I heard was that my activities and new boyfriend (at this age that's a funny term!) were interfering with the role others thought I should be living… that's what I heard.

Rather than ask questions and listen, my response, after a week of stewing, was a volcanic eruption, defending myself and not taking the opportunity to hear what was really going on. I damaged a precious relationship, and then had to work hard to create a bridge to repair it.

That is not who I want to be. In fact, it is the very antithesis of how I want to show up in this world. I have learned from that experience and even in the telling of it, have feelings of sadness…BUT, it gave me the jolt I needed to manage my emotions more effectively.

When you know who you are <u>not</u>, it's sometimes easier to gain clarity on who you are and who you want to become. You might also notice as you change, others around you may not like it. There is little comfort in change and little change in comfort. Others who care about you may even be getting in the way of your growth. It's one thing for us to change; it's another to deal with the change's others are making around us…or dealing with their response to our changes! You can't control the reactions of others. You have to let them manage that themselves. Sometimes relationships end or change drastically and we deal with those changes too. Life is a process and things are in constant flux. So be patient and insightful and know there may be resistance from others…it's part of the journey.

We may sometimes be so excited about our own growth and successes we want to engage those we love to come on the same journey. We may be disappointed or frustrated they don't share the same desire. Remember…you're only responsible for your own growth. You can support your loved ones and partners as they choose their own paths, but you cannot choose it for them. It is a huge relief when you can let that go.

Both of us have learned in our primary relationships that we cannot grow for our partners. In fact, if we trust them in their own growth, they will make the necessary changes in their own lives! We are not in control or in charge of anyone else…a thought both freeing and difficult at times!

We are all change-masters; we've just forgotten that we are! We came into this world from a cozy, warm, quiet place, kicking and screaming, but we did it beautifully. We learned how to deal with our environment in the most amazing way. We are still studying the incredible learning abilities of infants and young children; the abilities to learn as much as they need in order to manage in their strange new world.

That's us! **We're** the infants who've made all those changes, and we're not done yet. We went from the natural, unstructured learning environment of our home and neighbourhood (eating off the floors, manually dissecting caterpillars and sharing popsicles with our pet dogs) to the structured learning environment of school. That was a massive change! Some of us were kicking and screaming once again, but we did it! That became our "normal" world for many years. Even in that normal world we experienced change daily. We changed grades, friends, teachers; transitioned from printing to writing, from crayons to pens, and we did it seamlessly, one change melting into the next. Change was our natural world. Then we had to go out into the big world of work! Considering it was socially unacceptable to go kicking and screaming into that world, we hid our fear and changed again.

As we stand on the abyss of our next big change, we may forget how able we really are. We are "Change Masters". Sometimes our decisions worked out and sometimes it seemed like they didn't. When they didn't, we had the opportunity to learn and grow. We can become victims of what we may see as negative experiences or we can choose to use them as the gold mines of lessons, reflection, continuous learning and growth.

Try some of these techniques for self-reflection:

- Journal about a problem, or event and note your part in it. *Be honest with yourself about what happened and consider what you would like the final outcome to be.*
- Write a letter to your future self *and outline all your accomplishments.*
- Walk a labyrinth *with a specific focus*
- Light a candle, *sit and reflect*
- Meditate…*there are so many good meditation techniques*
- Visit a special place *where nature shows its beauty*
- Go for a quiet walk…*alone*

Possibility Mind Shift

What one thing can you do today to come closer to who you want to be?

If you wrote yourself a letter reflecting on the past year what would you say to yourself? If you think hard about it, you might recognize the challenges you have faced and overcome, the goals you have succeeded in meeting and the trials of day-to-day life you have managed. You could write about what you wish for yourself for the coming year, and identify your most important goals including those you feel motivated to attain.

For the past several years it has been our habit to write ourselves a letter. We do it early in January and date it to be opened on January 1 of the following year. In that letter we identify the things we want to work on, the challenges we are facing, as well as our hopes and dreams for the upcoming year. We also describe our successes and where we could have invested more attention to meet our goals. This reinforces the insights we have had, new perspectives we've learned and what our intentions are for the next steps in our journey.

Over the course of my adult life I can remember a handful of times when I was ashamed or felt guilty about my behaviour. On all these occasions I felt I had not lived according to my values and so had not been true to who I am. One of these times was when I was making the decision to end my first marriage. I had been unhappy for many years but only took the steps to end my marriage when I realized I didn't like the person I was becoming. I was angry and bitter, reminding myself of an older woman I knew well and certainly did not want to emulate. That realization allowed me to move forward into a new life recapturing who I really was.

On another occasion I reacted aggressively to someone who had clearly overstepped a boundary and invited a number of people to my home. However, I didn't register my concerns with her and she assumed it was acceptable. On the night of the event I unleashed my wrath in a very angry non-productive manner. The next day I became aware I had behaved in a way that did not sit comfortably with who I am. I made my apologies to all involved, even though the other party never acknowledged her role in this altercation. In order for me to feel good about myself, I put on my big girl panties and publicly took responsibility for my own actions.

I still think back to the lessons learned on these occasions and try to remember, even if I am angry, who I am at my core.

When you reflect on the changes you have made in the past few months, what change are you most proud of?

....

....

....

....

....

....

....

....

....

....

....

....

....

....

....

....

....

....

....

....

....

....

Think back to a time when you were uncomfortable with your behaviour. What is the lesson you have learned from this?

....

....

....

....

....

....

....

....

....

....

....

....

....

....

....

....

....

....

....

....

....

....

Week 20:

Celebration

The more you praise and celebrate your life,
the more there is in life to celebrate."
~ Oprah Winfrey ~

Take a minute and think back to the frog you met in Week One that was swimming in boiling water. We asked you way back then to rate your life satisfaction at that time. It's time to rate yourself again.

On a scale of one to ten, with ten being **AMAZING**, how do you rate your life now............

Celebrate! What do you notice about how far you've come?
How can you **celebrate** the changes you've made?

Too often we have a list of things to do; we successfully complete the tasks and happily cross them off the list. How often do we pay attention to and appreciate those accomplishments?

This module is all about taking some time to reflect and celebrate on how far you've come. It is about noticing the changes you've made and rewarding yourself for the work you've done.

Celebration can be something material, like a nice dinner out, a new dress, or flowers…or celebration can be sitting back and with slow, deep breaths and gratitude, drinking in the magnificent feeling of deep satisfaction and joy.

Celebration can simply be an appreciative awareness. It can be purposefully paying attention to what is working well. The intention is to really **NOTICE** and be grateful for what you have accomplished. We can so easily focus on the things that aren't going well and the problems left to be solved. Imagine what would happen if you started focusing on the things that are working, and celebrated both the small and the larger successes regularly. What if you focused more on what **feels** good and **is** good? Imagine your life becoming more satisfying and more rewarding daily.

Give yourself the gift of some reflective time to make a note of the growth edges you have exposed and that you're noticing some movement in. You've come a long way and you deserve to celebrate.

There are different and interesting opinions about why or why not celebrate. Here are some of the reasons people pass on celebration:

- I don't have time
- I don't know what to celebrate
- I want it to be meaningful but don't know how to make it so
- If I celebrate too much, I "lower the bar" (*yup…that's what someone said!*)
- I think about it, don't get to it and then it seems silly and it's too late anyway.

Challenge yourself to think about what and how you celebrate.

It's important to make the celebration **intentional** and **conscious**.
Really think about what you're honouring.
Make it sacred!

Make your own list of ways you would like to celebrate. By exploring those new ways you open new possibilities and opportunities and bring more of those things into your thoughts and your life. These celebrations can be private or shared, brief or time consuming …but will always be treasured moments.

- What would you like to celebrate?
- What stops you from celebrating?

*What type of ritual might you create to celebrate and honour **you** and your growth?*

"Celebrate what you want to see more of."
~ Thomas J. Peters~

This is also a time to consider what you need to leave behind. Everyone has had experiences they'd prefer not to have had, often hanging on to regrets and misgivings. Each of those experiences holds valuable lessons that make you a better person and certainly more equipped to move forward into new challenges. The lessons are weightless, but there can be baggage that weighs heavily. The baggage that's filled with guilt, blame, shame, remorse, "should haves" and "could haves" needs to be left behind. It's hard to celebrate while hanging on to all of that.

We challenge you to write a list of all that you want to leave behind, all the negative stuff that diminishes your energy and your power. Put it all down on paper…scribble all those negative thoughts onto as many pages as you need, and then ceremoniously crumple them up, put them in a fireplace and light a match! Watch them shrivel, shrink and disappear…and know you are now free to leave behind what you don't need. (*Caution! If you have enough pages to roast wieners or barbeque a steak you might want to try a safer ceremony…try burying the whole works, or maybe shredding it!!!*).

Now you're ready for the next leg of your journey, taking forward the joy of the lessons, the energy of the personal power of your successes, and the commitment to live bigger and better.

- What is one small thing you can do to pay more attention to your own successes?
- How will you continue to celebrate yourself and your accomplishments?

Notice how you acknowledge when you do well or when you reach a goal. Are you paying enough attention to your own success? What gets in your way? How will you stay true to your journey of growth and celebration?

I have worked with a young woman who trained as an African Shaman or a Sangoma. There is a ceremony practiced in that culture called a "River Washing", which celebrates the completion of one life stage. Depending on the stage being acknowledged, an appropriate river is chosen for the washing. The celebrant first faces downstream releasing the past and often giving the river a gift representing what has been learned and expressing gratitude for the learning. The individual then faces upstream greeting the future. The shaman has gathered some plants and medicines and mixes them with river water which is poured over the celebrant's head preparing her for the journey to come. It is a time of acknowledgment of successes, disappointments and other events from the past. It is also a time of joyful preparation for the events of the future. A pause in one's life between phases.

We can get caught up in our work and responsibilities and forget to celebrate the good things in our lives. Without celebrating what is going well we can fall into a trap of negativity.

By exploring new ways to celebrate you open new possibilities and opportunities to bring more of those things into your thoughts and your life.

*This is the last formal module in the **PMS** series. However, another module follows which provides additional random ideas, observations and opportunities for learning. We hope you have enjoyed your time with us and found it valuable. Please email us your thoughts about how this experience has impacted you and your life, and any other thoughts you'd like to share with us.*

*We encourage you to continue your journey into an even more enriching life experience. It doesn't have to end here...we invite you to start the **PMS** program again if you enjoyed it. It'll look and feel different the second time around.*

Remember life is a journey not a destination. We are honoured that you've shared a part of your journey with us...we'd love to go down the next path with you!

Thank you for growing with us...

Hilary and Anita

Our email addresses are:

hilarypms2020@gmail.com
anita2020pms@gmail.com

How can you celebrate your accomplishments and your successes?

....

....

....

....

....

....

....

....

....

....

....

....

....

....

....

....

....

....

....

....

....

....

....

....

How will you stay on your journey of growth and celebration?

....
....
....
....
....
....
....
....
....
....
....
....
....
....
....
....
....
....
....
....
....
....
....
....
....
....

Field Studies, Research Projects and Treasure Hunts
Any Week.... Every Week!

These activities are to keep you growing deeper into meaningful change,
and to keep you from charging on too fast!!!

This section is full of activities to support your treasure hunts, perspectives, reflections, discoveries, and actions. Whatever weekly module you are working on, try on some of these activities from the lens of wherever you are in your process. Each activity will likely look a little different from the perspective of each of the sections you are working on. It's better to do one of these activities rather than keep reading the next weekly module. These will help you deepen your learning, broaden your perceptions, and discover more ways to develop your growth in bigger ways. Mostly, have fun!

Enjoy the challenge and insights, and perhaps self-assess after each one you choose to engage in.

Your first project...what do you prefer to call these activities?

- Field Studies?
- Research Projects?
- Treasure Hunts?

Choose the word that you relate to and highlight that at the top of this page. What do you think your choice tells you about yourself?

Project #1:
Awakening and Shifting

PMS is about awakening. You're probably more awake than most if you're reading this. Have you noticed that some people are going through life half asleep? You might even find yourself in a state of complacency or on auto pilot, which isn't surprising because you, like most people, are busy just keeping yourself and your family fed, clothed and happy.

But just consider, **how "awake" are you?** On a scale of 1 – 10 (be honest with yourself!), how engaged are you? When was the last time you drank in the beauty of your surroundings, even if only the everyday surroundings you live in? When did you last notice the emotion in someone's eyes in addition to their verbal message, or looked at the night sky in wonder or just felt an explosion of joy for a moment in your day because you're so full of gratitude to be alive?

> *In the movie "**Awakening**", based on a true story, Leonard, played by Robert deNiro experiences the world for the first time after awakening from a 30-year catatonic state. He is mesmerized and amazed at what he sees and by what he is able to do. He is experiencing the joy of being alive, of moving through his day in absolute wonder at all there is newly available to him. As he experiences it himself, he also observes the rest of us and how we are responding in the world. He's puzzled and concerned…*
>
> *After realizing that he is slipping back into the prison of his catatonic state, and unable to sleep, he wanders through the halls of his institution. He calls his Doctor (played by Robin Williams) in the middle of the night, waking him with a frantic message that he needs to speak to him right now! When face to face with the bleary-eyed doctor, Leonard grabs a newspaper, slams it on the desk and yells look, LOOK!!! It's all bad! All they talk about is what's bad! You have to tell them…**tell them how wonderful life is!***

We can get consumed by negativity taking us down a road to unhappiness and depression. Life will continuously present us with problems and challenges – that is simply part of life. It can be easy to forget the good stuff at times, but there are ways to shift and move toward regeneration, appreciation and joy.

If you find yourself hanging on to your problems full time, you might try creating a "parking lot" for them.

- Put each problem on a small post it note and stick them on a wall in a closet while you do something fun or interesting without that problem on your mind. Then go back to the closet to revisit the problem with more energy and a new way of thinking about it.
- Write down what you "can" do within the limitations of the problem or challenge that is dogging you.

Search for two more creative ways to get past challenges and into position to cherish this amazing gift of life.

**Project #2:
"Make-Up for the Day"**

How different might your day be if you were to spend as much time and thought to how you will live it as you do on physically getting ready each morning? What might it look like to start each morning examining your true "make-up"? For instance, as you shower, could you consciously wash away yesterday's mistakes? You could let all the "could haves" and "should haves" go down the drain along with the mistakes leaving only the healthy glow of the wonderful lessons and benefits. Imagine those lessons as the essential oils of life soaking in through the pores.

As you apply your face cream you might consider that you are preparing for what is to come, recognizing the strength, sensitivity and the importance of the life you are preparing to live for this day.

As you apply your foundation, you might think about what the foundation is on which you will build this day, and subsequently your entire life. You might consider how you will be and what your intention is. This is your true "make-up". It represents the canvas on which you will paint your day and the backdrop for the life you bring uniquely to this world.

When you look in the mirror into your eyes give some thought to your vision and know where you are going today. Check your peripheral vision! There may be things coming up beside you that you need to be aware of and know you will see them without being taken off course. Clean your lenses and be sure they are the ones that bring the perspective you require for this day. They may need some adjustments to refocus, and a bit of a polish to remove the streaks that could impair your sight. What do you choose to see, and what do you want see?

Pay attention to your lips as you apply a colour! We challenge you to consider what is important to say and how you will speak your truth. Are your lips prepared to be impeccable with your word, and consider how those words might be received?

How will you prepare yourself for your next day?

How will you create yourself and your day to be the best it can be?

How are you living your life? So, what would it take for you to live past your fears and into greater life satisfaction?

Project #3:
Wagging or Barking

A friend sent a New Year's email message saying that her New Year's goal was to do more wagging and less barking. What an interesting concept!! So, in addition to fish and frogs, we're checking in to learn from the dogs!

It's interesting to think about how dogs typically respond. They might be barking with excitement or warning, wagging in delight or because they want to play or they might be napping and lazily peek out at us through drowsy eyelids preferring that calm and relaxed state!! Each of those behaviours uses energy differently and sets a tone for the environment and everyone in it. Imagine the energy it takes to be constantly reactive, on high alert and on guard, continuously making noise to defend and protect. It's tiring just to think of being so hyper-vigilant and interesting to think about how the rest of the world responds to that. How much comfort and humour can be enjoyed in that state? So, what can we learn from our canine friends about barking less and wagging more?

Wagging is the ability to receive pure enjoyment out of situations, to live in the moment and to be fully and positively engaged in the circumstances. It is the ability to enjoy the time spent with loved ones, taking pleasure in the small things and generally having more fun.

How much barking do you do in your life? How does it compare with the amount of wagging you do?

When you think about this creative perspective consider your most spontaneous reactions to situations. Many react by either barking or wagging without considering they have an option. Think about the last time you approached a difficult situation. Did you go in baring your teeth, snarling and barking in anger with a protective stance? Or did you approach the other person openly, with curiosity, eager to share or solve with respect, (maybe even with humour or 'wagging') to turn a difficult situation around?

When you next respond to a situation consider your response and just notice what you do.

- Did it work for you?
- Did you feel good about it?
- Were you barking or wagging?
- How do others respond to barking?
- How does their response work for you?

Project #4:
Dealing with Our Mistakes

It's no secret that we've all made mistakes. It's a great way to learn! But it's interesting to see how much we can get in the way of our own learning when we make a mistake and don't take responsibility for it. When we blame others or the circumstances rather than seek to find our part in the error, we miss the opportunity to grow.

How you feel about yourself and what happens to your relationships can be a high price to pay when mistakes are covered up and not "owned".

There was a video circulating several years ago by a young university professor who was dying of pancreatic cancer. He gave his last lecture to his students, not on his impending death, but rather with an inspiring presentation of his philosophy on living. One of the powerful messages in the video is the importance of recognizing your errors and apologizing when you do something wrong. He talks about the positive impact of taking responsibility for making the mistake, and then asking what you could do to correct it, or to make it right. This video is particularly moving and meaningful because he recorded it to leave for his three small children. It is a lasting legacy, a message about his perspective on the important things in life.

We don't have to be on death's door to get these important life lessons. We just need to be more aware. When people cover up their mistakes, they often end up feeling badly about themselves. They may feel a sense of shame and regret over long periods of time and may develop a continuously diminishing self-regard. These are unacceptable costs when you consider the lesser costs of 'fessing up, learning the lessons and living with integrity.

We all make mistakes. The learning comes from recognizing and admitting it, seeking the lesson, making some adjustments and not repeating the same mistakes. If we all did this just think of how much we could learn in a year!! Imagine the role models we would become for our children and the people around us.

What might you do differently the next time you make a mistake? What is stopping you?

Project #5:
Fear or Excitement?

What would you do if you weren't afraid? Have you ever noticed that the physical symptoms of fear and excitement are similar?

> *A little girl was afraid of flying and told her Mom that she really didn't want to go to visit Grandma if she had to go by plane. Her Mom asked her how she felt about flying. She answered that she had butterflies in her stomach, she couldn't breathe deeply, she had trouble swallowing and couldn't sleep. Her Mom asked how she felt when she was going to Disneyland last year. She replied that she was excited. "And how did that feel?" asked her Mom. She described exactly the same symptoms!*

So, with this awareness can we actually "choose" fear or excitement? Maybe so, if we can get past our self-limiting thoughts and behaviours… "feel the fear and do it anyway", which is also the name of a great book by Susan Jeffers and it's a Nike commercial!

Each of us has had the experience of limiting what we do or diminishing ourselves and our lives because of our fears. We may be afraid of making a mistake, looking silly or somehow failing. We may have a fear of not measuring up and some may even be afraid to succeed!

We seem to be painfully aware of our shortcomings and too often forget to acknowledge our strengths and what we have to offer. There may have been a time when in a group you held back with a response to someone's question or didn't engage in a discussion because you second guessed yourself. Or perhaps there was a time when you were invited to participate alongside someone you had great respect for and refused because you thought you wouldn't measure up or might disappoint.

Mark Twain wrote "*Dance like nobody's watching; love like you've never been hurt. Sing like nobody's listening; live like it's heaven on earth.*" So, what is it that's getting in your way?

To live a life of few regrets we need to become aware of our opportunities and our choices. We need to know our comfort zone, fears, limitations and strengths, where we can stretch, and how to be safe when we do.

Consider what it would take for you to live with a bit more courage to overcome your self-imposed barriers. Create a habit of remembering your strengths and successes that have carried you through challenges. As you live more fully you have more opportunities to contribute to the world. Your contribution may help someone else have greater insight, a new perspective or maybe your participation will give someone else the confidence to do the same.

What opportunities have you missed that you regret?

What would you do differently next time?

How will you know when you have arrived at the place you really want to be in your life?

Project #6:
Worrying

How much energy do you spend worrying about things that may never happen or things you can do nothing about?

How many of us spend our days worrying about everything? We worry about the past; what we should have said and done, how we should have managed that difficult conversation (that'd be *Medulla the Duck!*), and if the result was the best we could have done. We worry about the future; how we will handle this new situation, how our family members will respond to whatever, what will happen when…add your own worry here! We worry about things that do not matter; like what someone will think of our messy kitchen counter when they drop in for a visit, or if our child will win the spelling contest. We worry about things we can do nothing about, like how bad the traffic will be on the way home or if our flights will connect as they should.

It might be interesting to choose not to worry for one week and see what happens. Notice what it is like to replace worry with an acknowledgement of thanks for the lessons of the past, and then either plan or do something for those events in the present or future. Let go of the worries of the past, it is history and cannot be changed. The past is there to learn from so you can accept your lessons and move forward to make better choices the next time. Choose to replace the worries of the future with an action; doing something about the things you can and then letting the rest go. Instead of worrying about what others may do, allow them to experience their own consequences and let the future unfold without getting in the way.

There was a woman who chose to limit her worry time to only 15 minutes a day at seven pm. The rest of the day she would put off the worry until that time, and when she sat down to worry, it seemed like a very ridiculous thing to do!

Think about what your life would be like if you let go of all the petty little worries occurring every day. Those will be the worries stealing your time and energy that you will not even remember in a week. Imagine what you might accomplish if you used your worry time to do something more productive, something that really matters.

What do you worry about? What will it take for you to let those worries go?

Project #7:
Self Care

How do you look after yourself?

Do you feel "burnt out", "on the edge" or do you talk about your stress frequently? Is it the story you're telling yourself and others that is keeping you stuck, or is it the truth that you need to manage?

> *Ann puts everyone else in her life first. She has a young family with many needs and a husband who always relies on her help. Her parents and other family members count on her to arrange social activities for them, buy gifts and generally organize important events. She works full time and volunteers in the community. Ann often feels overwhelmed by even trying to take the time to have a few minutes to herself. As a result, she is becoming short tempered with her family, doesn't perform as effectively at work and feels undervalued by everyone in her life.*

Does this sound familiar? How are you modeling "self-care" for your children? Many people find that they cannot put themselves first in their lives. If they stopped to consider what they are demonstrating to their children and others in their lives it may shift their behaviours. It's important to develop new perspectives and strategies to manage the busy demands of life and find ways to form new habits. Consider how we learned about life balance. Did your parents model a nice balance of work, leisure, relaxation, and self-care? Not likely! What messages did you take away from that and how have you implemented those ideas in your life?

Self-care can be as simple as taking the time to sit and enjoy the outdoors for a few minutes before making a meal. It can involve a weekend away at a spa, regular exercise, taking the time to meet a friend for coffee or simply taking a short walk. The habit of looking after yourself becomes easier to maintain once you start to enjoy the benefits. But some may misinterpret this message...we have to be careful that self-care doesn't tip over into selfishness!

How important are **you** in the priorities of your busy life? Once you find that self-care magic, how are you giving that to others in your life? Sharing the best of who you are with those you care about is the legacy that you live and leave!

What one small thing can you start doing now that will provide you with a self-care activity to help you feel more balanced?

Project #8:
More Medulla the Duck

Voices in your head? Yes! We all have them and we are not talking about external voices, we are talking about how you talk to yourself!!

Robert K. Cooper, a neuroscience pioneer and leadership advisor, talks about an area at the base of the brain known as the medulla, a vital link to the reticular activating system or RAS. The RAS connects the major nerves in the spinal column and brain, sorting out the many million impulses that the brain must deal with each second.

This part of the brain has evolved over the millennia with an inherent tendency to magnify negative incoming messages and minimize the positive ones.

This was a useful thing for hunters long ago when we needed to be critically aware of the things in our environments that could hurt or kill us. This part of our brain no longer plays such a useful role as it keeps us on alert to negative thoughts or potential threats we may encounter. We call this warning voice "Medulla the Duck". Okay, so now we've added ducks to the fish, frogs and dogs to learn from! That duck is the inner voice that keeps us much too well informed of our supposed "dangers" and "limitations". That duck saps our energy, keeps us focused on the negative and diminishes our confidence and ability. It is now a barrier and we think it is time to **shut the duck up**!

How is that duck showing up for you in your life? Do you find yourself listening to negative self-talk in your head, that pesky voice telling you, "Who do you think you are?" "What do you think you are doing in this project or group?" "That was a dumb thing to say...I'm such an idiot"! You name what the duck is saying to you!!

We challenge you to start paying attention to that quacking. Notice the tone in which you talk to yourself and the types of things you say. If you find the messages are negative and nasty, then work on shutting it up!!

What is that duck saying to you? How can you become more aware of the quacking and learn to change the negative messages into positive ones?

Project #9:
Watch Your Language!

What would happen if we REALLY paid attention to our own language, both the voice in our head and the one that makes a noise?

How many times a day do you catch yourself saying "I have to" or "I should"?

Sometimes that language is appropriate, but it could be a habit that is having a negative impact.

Our thoughts create our language, and our language frames our orientation in the world. If you are truly feeling that you "have to" do something, it sounds like that something may not be your choice! Knowing we have choices is important for a healthy emotional state, yet the language we use can be sending unintended messages that diminish our emotional well-being. The words you use may be creating a negative response or feeling, holding you unintentionally in a "victim" mindset.

How often do you say "I should"? You likely have said it many times. It's a phrase that diminishes our self-esteem by reminding us of what we didn't do. "I should have said" this or that, or "I should have done" something else! It's a subtle and effective way to beat yourself up. You just can't win at that game because it can never turn out differently considering it would involve changing the past! One of our favourite sayings is "don't should on yourself". Instead, a more positive and self-supportive statement is one that indicates what you have learned from the past and what you will do in similar circumstances in the future.

The future tense of this same phrase leaves you continuously feeling like you can't and aren't measuring up. I "should do" something sends a "nagging" message, and who likes to be nagged? What if you were to catch yourself in action and instead use a phrase that brings you into a stronger level of confidence and control? Try using a few other words and phrases that might be more positive. For instance, try out "I choose to", "I want to" or "I will". *And then take steps to DO IT!!!*

An exercise to demonstrate the power of language is to write on the top of a page "Things I Have to Do This Week" and then continue to create a complete list. When you are finished, cross out "Have to" and replace it with "Choose to". What is the difference in how you are feeling about that list?

We challenge you to count the number of times you use these words and phrases?

Just become aware of these habits…and remember, don't "should" on yourself!

There is research suggesting that the brain thinks in positive language and images.

This means that when you say either internally or out loud something like, "I will not smoke", your brain processes it as, "I **will** smoke", eliminating or ignoring the negative. The brain dismisses the negative which obviously changes the message drastically! Could it be that if instead of saying "I will not smoke" we said "I am now committed to breathing clean air", our focus would shift from smoking to breathing well?

You may have noticed many young children who reach for the brightly coloured items in the supermarket. You then may have heard the parents saying "don't touch!" along with other reprimands that don't seem to be working very well. Considering this research, the child's brain is processing the word "touch"! We already know this doesn't work very well, but not many have changed the approach over the years. Recently someone was surprised to witness a young mother break the pattern. Her response to small hands that dropped a bottle of ketchup in the aisle was "please put your hands in your lap" and the child immediately did so. What a wonderful example of giving a clear message that didn't confuse the child. It was clear and directive rather than confused by a negative message. We need to give a clear message for the brain to more directly interpret.

Changing your eating regime for health or weight loss? "I can't have cookies because I am on a diet" sends a message of loss and restriction. Is it possible to change it to something like "I'm choosing a healthy lifestyle with yummy fruits and healthy snacks to feel better"? Which is more motivating and self-supportive?

Think hard about how your language may be affecting your outcomes and how you think about things. Notice how many negatives you are using in your internal dialogue and with others in your life?

Our language can have a huge impact on our experience. If we become aware of the words that we use, we can create an opportunity to change our experience. A very talented young woman uses the word "hate" in her vocabulary quite often. She reports that she hates certain types of people, activities and experiences. Just by using this word she is inadvertently pushing people away with the intensity of the emotion around it. She doesn't realize the negative impact she's having on her relationships and outcomes simply through her language.

Project #10:
Making Stuff Up

Have you ever caught yourself saying something and then realized you are generalizing or actually making stuff up about something that may not even be true?

Comments like: "She is mad at me!! I can tell by the way she ignored me yesterday."

How can you know what the other person is feeling? Have they told you they are mad at you or are you assuming that by their body language or other clues?

Or how about, "He never listens to me!!" Is it the truth or does he **sometimes** listen when you are talking? With a statement like that, you are likely generalizing! Your brain is believing what you are saying, and you are creating a false belief!

Can you think of a time when you jumped to a conclusion about how someone was feeling and then assumed you were correct? Remember it is rarely all about us!! If someone seems distracted, maybe they aren't mad at you but rather have a pressing personal problem on their minds. If someone speaks to you in a loud tone, maybe they are used to having to raise their voice to be heard and don't even realize what they are doing. Perhaps the person who cut in front of you in traffic isn't just a jerk, but is actually reacting to a family emergency and needs to get home to a crisis? That would be what we call a most respectful interpretation or MRI. Then let it go!

What assumptions are you making about what people say to you? How might that be limiting?

Over the next week pay attention to the words you use in your day to day interactions. Are you mind-reading what others are thinking without really knowing what is going on for them? Are you making stuff up and then creating a reality around the made-up stuff?

Project #11:
Tough Conversations

When we were growing up many of us heard our parent's say, "If you can't say anything nice don't say anything at all."

Although this can be good advice, and this wisdom serves us well in many circumstances, there can be a cost to it. In all things there needs to be balance and common sense involved to make the wisdom become wise! You may be in a situation where you consistently feel unheard. Sometimes you've tried being "nice" and it's not getting the kind of results or relationships you need or want. What if being nice is actually being dishonest? We sometimes must be respectfully honest when nice isn't working.

The costs of stress related illness are rising. Although we don't fully understand the correlation between stress and illness it is obvious when stress is unresolved there is a cost to our health. We all know people who have some type of illness that becomes worse by unresolved conflict and stress. Many of us have been negatively affected by the worry taking a toll on our health.

Think about a time you have handled difficult situations in the past. How did your body react? It may show up as digestive upsets, or a restricted throat with headaches or back pain. Listen carefully to see what your body is trying to tell you. The cues our bodies are giving us can help us more quickly identify when we need to move to action. We can do something to resolve the situation earlier or wait until we get an unmistakable message from our body that something is seriously wrong. Pay attention to the early signs and act on them.

How does your body tell you when there is something you need to pay attention to? Listen to your body…it's trying to tell you something. What tough conversation do you need to have?

And by the way, you don't need to choose "nice" or "ugly", you can choose respectfully honest!

Possibility Mind Shift

Project #12:
Conversation with Older, Wiser Self

What made us so good at managing change in our past? Each of us may have different answers, but many might come up with something like agility and flexibility…yes, we are adaptable. And what about adventurous and optimistic? Our childhood curiosity took us into the darnedest places where we learned our best stuff! And aren't we resourceful and courageous? Didn't we come up with the most amazing ways to make and do things? That's how we gained the confidence to get up every day into a world we didn't know and do what we had to do. And that is still who we are. We are still agile and flexible (maybe not as much in our bodies as in our minds!), we are adaptable, adventurous and optimistic, and curious and resourceful. We just have to remember who and what we are so we can once again be courageous and confident to meet our changing future head on. We can do it because we are good at it. We are change masters!

At times the day to day problems we face can seem overwhelming and insurmountable. We may be thrown off by simple mistakes or an overwhelming bill and feel that we will never be able to climb back out of the hole we have made for ourselves. A strategy that has worked well for some people is to consider if the problem being faced right now will be important in a year. Will it still be a problem? Is it long forgotten? Or are there serious ramifications from it?

Asking these questions may help put what seems like an overwhelming problem into perspective.

Imagine you could have a conversation with your older wiser self. Choose an age that feels wise to you and imagine what this wiser self would say to the person you are today. How important is the problem that is overwhelming to you now when you look at it from the perspective of the future? Close your eyes and imagine yourself at 90 years of age. Become that person, the person you will be, wise and honest. You are looking back at your life with humour, admiration and satisfaction. Your younger self (who you are now) has asked your advice about the challenges being faced today and you (the wise one) is writing this letter to give some sagely advice.

What advice is that older, wiser self giving you? What do you need to consider? What do you need to let go of? What holds great importance?

Possibility Mind Shift

Project #13:
Creating Your Future

Is it an excuse or the truth?

It seems that many of us work and strive to get "somewhere". We tell ourselves that when the mortgage is paid off, or when the children are grown, or when we retire, things will be different and we will be where we really want to be. But what does "there" look like? How will you know when you have arrived at your destination?

The often-told quote of "life being a journey not a destination" comes to mind and although we know this intellectually, how many really live it? We talk about how our lives would change if we won the lottery and philosophize about how we would choose differently if we only had a month to live. But be honest with yourself. Is it really money or a time crunch that would force you into the perfect life? What would you honestly do differently if you could create the life you would truly find satisfying?

Think about what your life will look like when you arrive at the place you are working towards. Know what your average day will be like in that imagined time in the future. What are you waiting for? Get clear and know what you are working toward so you will know when you get there!

We see people striving for that "magical" time in the future, and we also see people looking back with fondness about their past. A life lived in the past or in the future is a life wasted, so remember every day there is something to appreciate that is part of the journey to "there".

What are you not doing while waiting for "ideal circumstances"? What CAN you do to make a small difference that will grow into a big difference?

 I was busy with teenagers, working and going to school, but really wanted to find some time to capture the stories of my aging parents on my brand new laptop! They were in their 80's and I didn't want to miss out on the lessons and the interesting specifics of their lives. Although we saw each other nearly every weekend for a family dinner, it was such a noisy, busy time with so many of us that it wasn't the right time for capturing those details. I called them to make arrangements to meet and capture their memoirs. Turns out it was hard to find time in our busy schedules...they were busy dancing three times a week and bowling once a week...still so busy living their lives and creating memories that they didn't have lots of time to capture them!!! That was lesson number one from their memoirs! Live every day...now...and enjoy your life... now!!! What remarkable people with amazing lessons for living. I did end up capturing many of their stories, along with so many more great examples to share.

Possibility Mind Shift

And just for the record...

You might find it interesting to know that we actually do "eat our own cookies" so to speak! As we were editing this book we caught ourselves making an assumption about an event that was foremost in our minds. We were "making stuff up" just when we were editing the "Making Stuff Up" piece in the Field Studies segment! Our discussion included "but I didn't make stuff up intentionally!" YES! That's exactly the point...we don't do this stuff intentionally! It happens through habit, conditioning, and limited perspective over time. We had a great laugh and then decided that we had to share that moment with you. This isn't a purely intellectual process.

Just because you have read this and "get it", and have even put it to good use, doesn't mean you've "arrived". None of us "arrive". There is no finish line...except if you're wearing a "toe tag"! Sorry for the dark humour, but it's the truth.

This is a continuous, sometimes difficult and often humourous journey into the future. So have fun on the trip and don't beat yourself up if you catch yourself in a bad habit...you are human after all and you get to have a chance at finding yet another lesson to make the next thing more interesting and the right thing for you!

Bibliography

Baldwin, Christina. Storycatcher: making sense of our lives through the power and practice of story. New World Library, 2005.

Chapman, Gary. The Five Love Languages: How to Express Heartfelt Commitment to your mate. Northfield Publishing, 2004.

Doyle, Glennon. Untamed. The Dial Press, 2020.

Elkin, Bruce. Simplicity and Success: Creating the Life you long for. Trafford Publishing, 2003.

Golman, Daniel. Social Intelligence: The New Science of Human Relationships. Bantam Books, 2006.

Hanson, Rick and Mendius, Richard. The Practical Neuroscience of Buddha's Brain, Happiness, love and wisdom. New Harbinger Publications, 2009.

Katherine, Anne. Boundaries: where you end and I begin. Fireside, 2000.

Kondo, Marie. The life-changing magic of tidying up: the Japanese art of decluttering and organizing. Ten Speed Press, 2014.

Lombard, Annemarie. Sensory Intelligence: Why it matters more than EQ and IQ. Metz Press, 2018.

Milburn, Joshua Fields. Minimalism: Live a Meaningful life. Asymmetrical Press, 2016.

Scott, Susan. Fierce Conversations: Achieving Success in work and in life, one conversation at a time. New American Library, 2017.

Zander, Benjamin and Zander, Rosamund. The Art of Possibility: Transforming personal and professional life. Harvard Business School Press, 2000.

About the Authors

When **Anita Bakker** and **Hilary Drummond** connected in the early 2000's it felt like a long friendship rediscovered. They shared values, interests and as newly Certified Executive Coaches from Royal Roads University in British Columbia, were excited to partner on many projects. They found a particular passion for working with and helping other women have richer and more satisfying lives. Through the development of a variety of workshops and projects including "Wine, Women and Song", "Wise Women Weekend", and "Change in Mind" the first edition of **Possibility Mind Shift** or "**PMS**" was born. They created a web based coaching program, had a weekly newspaper column, worked with professional women in organizations and individuals as coaching clients. They found that bringing humour and laughter to the process enriched the deep reflective learning. From these experiences **PMS** has become richer and fuller from their own Coaching practices as well as the feedback of their clients.

CPSIA information can be obtained
at www.ICGtesting.com
Printed in the USA
BVHW022104150221
600191BV00001B/1